Regional Governance and
the Politics of Housing in
the San Francisco Bay Area

T0097831

Regional Governance and the Politics of Housing in the San Francisco Bay Area

Paul G. Lewis and
Nicholas J. Marantz

TEMPLE UNIVERSITY PRESS

Philadelphia • *Rome* • *Tokyo*

TEMPLE UNIVERSITY PRESS
Philadelphia, Pennsylvania 19122
tupress.temple.edu

Library of Congress Cataloging-in-Publication Data

Names: Lewis, Paul George, 1966– author. | Marantz, Nicholas J., 1979–
  author.
Title: Regional governance and the politics of housing in the San Francisco
  Bay Area / Paul G. Lewis, Nicholas J. Marantz.
Other titles: Political lessons from American cities.
Description: Philadelphia : Temple University Press, 2023. | Series:
  Political Lessons from American Cities | Includes bibliographical
  references and index. | Summary: "Analyzes how the structure of
  government in the San Francisco Bay Area complicates efforts to address
  the region's housing shortage and identifies options for reform, drawing
  larger lessons about the dangers of fragmented local authority"—
  Provided by publisher.
Identifiers: LCCN 2022040341 (print) | LCCN 2022040342 (ebook) | ISBN
  9781439923603 (cloth) | ISBN 9781439923610 (paperback) | ISBN
  9781439923627 (pdf)
Subjects: LCSH: Metropolitan government—California—San Francisco Bay
  Area. | Housing development—Government policy—California—San
  Francisco Bay Area. | Housing policy—California—San Francisco Bay
  Area. | Land use—Government policy—California—San Francisco Bay Area.
  | San Francisco Bay Area (Calif.)—Politics and government.
Classification: LCC JS451.C28 S356 2023 (print) | LCC JS451.C28 (ebook) |
  DDC 353.5/5097946—dc23/eng/20221122
LC record available at https://lccn.loc.gov/2022040341
LC ebook record available at https://lccn.loc.gov/2022040342

Printed in the United States of America

9 8 7 6 5 4 3 2 1

Contents

Acknowledgments

The research that underlies this book would not have been possible without the support of the Emmett Shear Charitable Trust. We are grateful to Emmett Shear and Ken Shear for encouraging us to investigate the possible influence of jurisdictional size on housing policy in the Bay Area, for asking probing questions, and for allowing us the intellectual freedom to take the study wherever it led us.

Richardson Dilworth, series editor of Political Lessons from American Cities, was very receptive to our project and had excellent ideas about how to tailor the book to the series and its intended audience. We also have enjoyed working with Aaron Javsicas and his highly professional team at Temple University Press. TUP engaged two very perceptive anonymous reviewers, who provided suggestions and asked questions that led to significant improvements in the final product. We received additional helpful input from Scott Bollens, Alejandro Camacho, Albert Solé-Ollé, and Christopher Acuff. Views and conclusions expressed in this book, as well as any errors, are the responsibility of the authors and do not represent the funder or any of the aforementioned individuals.

Most of all, we thank our families for their patience, support, and good humor.

Regional Governance and
the Politics of Housing in
the San Francisco Bay Area

Introduction

Linking the Bay Area's Structure
of Governance to Its Housing Crisis

Housing shortages afflict many metropolitan regions in the United States, particularly in coastal states with vibrant job markets. For residents of such regions—particularly households with low or moderate incomes—housing costs often are extremely burdensome. Nowhere is the housing crisis more pronounced than in the San Francisco Bay Area, generally considered the most expensive regional housing market in the country. In the two decades beginning in 2000, the Bay Area added jobs and residents at a much more rapid pace than it added housing, as the number of new residential units built lagged well below the number that had been built in earlier periods. From 2011 to 2017 alone, during a period of sustained economic recovery from the Great Recession, the region added 4.7 jobs for every one new unit of housing. This lack of housing production contributed to an escalation of rents and home prices, and the ratio was worse in many parts of the region where job growth was high. Meanwhile, the income gap between the Bay Area's richest and poorest residents widened considerably.[1] Not surprisingly, then, by 2017 nearly one-third of the households in the Bay Area region were considered excessively cost burdened by housing, spending more than 35 percent of their income on shelter. Rates were far worse among lower-income households and people of color.[2]

Policy makers, activists, and scholars have proposed a plethora of diagnoses and remedies for such housing shortages and inequities. Rarely, however, have they made systematic connections between patterns of housing development and the structure of governance in a region—that is, the institutional arrangements by which a metropolis is governed. Lack of attention to that connection between government structure and housing outcomes, we argue, is a lamentable oversight—one we aim to remedy in this book. The architecture of government in a region influences political power and land-use decision-making in ways that systematically shape the built environment—including the development, or lack of development, of housing.

In the San Francisco Bay Area, a region of 7.7 million residents, there are 101 municipalities, nine counties, and several regional agencies that hold varied responsibilities.[3] The municipalities—commonly called *cities* in California, regardless of size—hold the primary role in land-use policy, creating the plans, zoning ordinances, and subdivision regulations that govern what can be built where. Cities are the primary units of local government in the region, controlling land-use regulation as well as key public services such as policing for the 90.7 percent of Bay Area residents who live within city boundaries.[4] This highly decentralized structure of governance affects the region's ability to increase its residential supply and pursue a regional vision for equitable housing opportunity. In particular, as we demonstrate, small-scale cities—of which the Bay Area has many—generally have a built-in bias against multifamily housing development. Meanwhile, the Bay Area's region-wide agencies, ostensibly designed to handle problems of metropolitan scale, lack sufficient leverage or motivation to effectively reshape the region's future growth. Our book focuses on this broad, nine-county region because its housing and land-use problems are not limited to the big cities of San Francisco, Oakland, and San Jose. Instead, these problems—and their causes—are metropolitan in scale.[5]

A Case in Point: Localism in Lafayette and a Regional Response

In one indication of the severity of the Bay Area's housing crisis, a previously obscure civil servant took a stand in 2018 that has become almost legendary among those who pay attention to the region's housing shortage. In the fall of that year, Steven Falk decided that he'd had enough.[6] Falk was the longtime city manager of Lafayette, an affluent suburb of twenty-six thousand residents about sixteen miles northeast of San Francisco (see Figure I.1). He believed that permitting multifamily housing near his city's Bay Area Rapid Transit (BART) station would be the best way for Lafayette to address the challenges of housing affordability, income inequality, and climate change. But in the face of sustained opposition to such projects from the voters and elected officials to whom he answered, Falk resigned. He also posted his resignation letter on Twitter, writing, "It has become increasingly difficult for

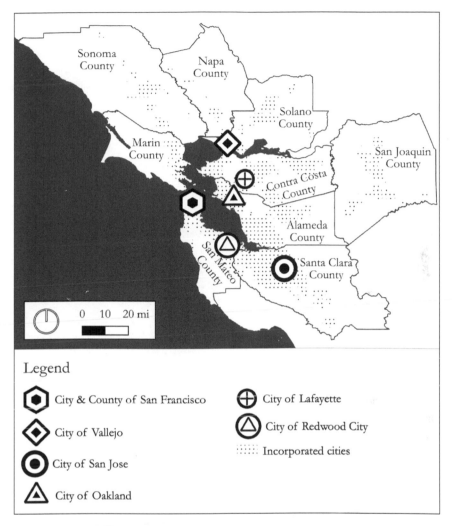

Figure I.1 The San Francisco Bay Area The region customarily is defined to include the nine counties (including San Francisco) surrounding the San Francisco Bay. However, many long-distance commuters to Bay Area jobs reside in San Joaquin County and other inland areas.

me to support, advocate for, or implement policies that would thwart transit density. My conscience won't allow it."[7]

However, Falk's vision of transit-oriented, multifamily housing in Lafayette may yet become a reality. Just days after Falk announced his resignation, California governor Gavin Newsom signed legislation that would take some power over land-use regulation out of Lafayette's hands. In order to promote a regional plan for dense residential development around transit stations, which had been adopted by the BART district, the new state law required local land-use regulation to accommodate the development envisioned in the BART plan on BART-owned property. One such property eyed by BART for transit density was the parking lot adjacent to the Lafayette station.[8]

The case of Lafayette illustrates an important lesson: Highly localized control of land use can thwart housing development in locations where it would be most beneficial. And small suburban cities like Lafayette are more likely to be part of the problem than to embrace a solution to the housing shortage. But the case also hints at the potential for regionalized decision-making authority to help address the challenges of climate change, income inequality, and housing affordability. If cities like Lafayette had less final authority to veto housing proposals, a more regionally beneficial housing development pattern might result. For example, under BART's plan, parts of the parking lots that currently adjoin rail stations in communities like Lafayette could be developed as mid-rise housing and office space.[9] Expanding the supply of market-rate and subsidized housing would help reduce the rate of increase in the region's housing costs.[10] Increasing the amount of transit-adjacent housing and office space could mitigate congestion on roadways. And providing housing in this relatively close-in location, accessible to some of the region's biggest concentrations of jobs, could reduce the need for lengthy auto commutes, which are responsible for an increasing share of California's greenhouse gas emissions.

But BART's plan only applies to the relatively small amount of land that BART owns. How will more sustainable and affordable development patterns emerge in the face of often vigorous local opposition? Strengthened regional institutions, bolstered by supportive state government legislation, will be necessary to overcome antihousing localism.

A Preview of Our Argument

This book explains how the governmental geography of the Bay Area—with its plethora of communities like Lafayette that have a veto power over residential proposals—contributes to the region's housing shortage. In Chapter 1, we argue that small-population municipalities are generally less amenable to housing development—especially new multifamily housing—than large municipalities, and we describe several reasons why this would be the case. Chapter 1 also explores the historical origins of the Bay Area's fragmented system of local government and the likely influence of that structure on housing development patterns.

Chapter 2 tests our claim empirically, examining the relationship between jurisdictional population size and housing outcomes during the period of recovery after the Great Recession. Results of our statistical analysis, which looks at multifamily development among local governments in California's metro areas, suggest that small jurisdictional size is linked to subpar rates of increase in multifamily housing. We then show that small municipalities dominate the landscape in many of the Bay Area's most job-rich locations. These job-rich areas are highly appropriate for multifamily, mixed-use, and transit-oriented development but have been largely a dead zone for new housing, experiencing little or no recent increase in multifamily units. With potential infill housing displaced from such communities, workers often find that the housing they can afford is located instead at the auto-dependent far fringes of the region.

If the Bay Area's localized system of land-use control is not providing housing that the region needs, could geographically more inclusive governmental organizations counter these negative effects? After all, as "regional citizens," residents lack a political unit or election where they can register their concerns about area-wide problems such as housing availability or long-distance commutes. The latter part of Chapter 2 summarizes how several generations of reformers have attempted to create a regional level of government capable of shaping the Bay Area's development patterns. As we show, while the Bay Area today has no shortage of region-wide *governmental institutions*, it is not regionally *governed*: None of the metropolitan-level entities created to date has strong leverage over housing and land-use patterns. Thus, to many residents of the region, the Bay Area's growth patterns and housing outcomes seem, literally and figuratively, out of control.

If there is a partial exception to this lack of control, it involves those residents fortunate enough to already own homes in relatively small, well-off communities like Lafayette, who seek—often successfully—to minimize land-use changes in their immediate area. Restrictive land-use regulation in close-in cities such as Lafayette reinforces historic inequities, contributing to enduring patterns of ethno-racial segregation and unequal access to opportunities. Even the power enjoyed by residents of affluent suburbs in shaping their communities is only partial, however, since the lack of sufficient housing development near employment means that their roads often become congested by commuters from far-off residential communities. And the absence of affordable local housing opportunities means that local-serving businesses and schools in the affluent communities often have trouble attracting and retaining the employees upon whom residents depend.

In short, the system of land-use control in the Bay Area is highly fragmented—divided in such a way as to impede government's ability to improve the housing situation. In Chapter 3, therefore, we evaluate the Bay Area's structure of regional governance in the context of recent discussions—in the region, in California state government, and nationally—about how to improve land-use regulation. Specifically, we provide a menu of possible options to improve housing opportunity through reforms in government structure or the enactment of state legislation, ranging from incremental to more radical. In contrast to prior generations of would-be reformers who pressed for sweeping changes to regional government structure, we argue that more targeted reforms of local and regional institutions could generate durable improvements to the sustainability of the region's growth pattern.

Finally, the Conclusion draws together the main lessons from the case of the San Francisco Bay Area and offers some strategic considerations that policy makers and housing advocates should consider. Strategy is important to achieve effective reform. And without such reform, housing stability and economic mobility for workers and families who try to make a home in job-rich regions like the Bay Area will continue to be an elusive goal.

A Fragmented System
of Land-Use Governance

afayette, California, where city manager Steven Falk resigned due to his city's unwillingness to accommodate multifamily housing, is a geographically fortunate community, located near the heart of one of the most economically dynamic urban regions in the world. Yet despite its proximity to large and expanding job centers, Lafayette remains a small, quiet suburb characterized mainly by single-family homes. Throughout the twenty-first century, Lafayette's population has barely budged. Its average annual increase was a barely perceptible 86 people (or less than 0.4 percent) from 2000 to 2020, according to population estimates from the California Department of Finance. Residential growth was sluggish despite Lafayette's advantageous accessibility by road and rail to many of the Bay Area's growing job centers.

Might Lafayette's smallness be related to its slow growth? Yes. The low population of cities like Lafayette can contribute to a lack of enthusiasm for housing the workers who help create the Bay Area's economic vitality. And, by extension, the fact that Lafayette is merely one of 101 municipalities in the Bay Area, most of them fairly small, contributes to the housing shortfall in the region. The median population size of municipalities in the region as of 2020 was 31,439—just a shade larger than Lafayette. In total, 63 of the region's 101 cities had populations below fifty thousand.[1]

Certainly, other factors influence the limited supply and high cost of housing in the Bay Area, such as the region's complex topography of hills and waterways and the increasing presence of highly paid tech workers who can afford to spend a lot on housing. But in the expensive coastal regions of

California, "the biggest obstacle to new housing is localized opposition, which manifests itself as strict zoning, cumbersome approval processes, and/or local activism against new development."[2] Here we focus on an oft-overlooked element of such opposition to new housing: the small scale of the jurisdictions making decisions about the use of land.

Why Small Local Governments May Be Particularly Likely to Hinder Housing

In small-population suburbs, homeowners tend to hold political primacy, given their relatively large share of the voting population. Furthermore, for most homeowners, their home is their largest investment.[3] Economist William Fischel describes such homeowners as *homevoters*, because their participation in local affairs centers around protecting housing values.[4] In the view of Fischel and other scholars, homevoters worry that the addition of new housing development nearby—especially large-scale housing development—would introduce unwanted competition in the home-sale market. Unlike renters, Monkkonen and Manville note, "home owners are both consumers and *capitalists*. In their role as capitalists, they have incentives to behave like producers in any other market, and protect the value of their assets by restricting new entrants"—that is, new housing units.[5] Homevoters also may fear that new housing will bring disruptions to their neighborhoods, in the form of school crowding, increased traffic, or parking problems, for example.[6]

In small municipalities like Lafayette, homeowners and members of their households often constitute a large majority of the electorate. Their concerns about home values and potential neighborhood disruption are thus very likely to find an outlet in local politics and a receptive ear from local elected officials. Longtime residents are particularly concerned about the proximity of proposed new housing, particularly multifamily housing, and the scale of land-use decision-making in small suburbs can reflect and even amplify those concerns. In small communities, as compared with larger cities, homeowners are less likely to see their political influence counterbalanced by developers, large employers, and other progrowth political interests.[7] To put it another way, small jurisdictions tend to define their community's self-interest and goals quite narrowly.[8]

In small suburbs, moreover, homeowners' advantages in political organizing are particularly strong. Homeowners find it relatively easy to coalesce in a small community, often getting to know each other through involvement in their children's school, as the quality of local schools is also a central preoccupation in many suburbs. Moreover, school quality is indirectly connected to house values, since schools are supported by taxes on property wealth and perceived school quality affects home prices.

A corollary to this perspective suggests that large-population municipalities are more likely than small ones to allow new housing, particularly multifamily developments. Changing the scale of decision-making by placing land-use decisions in a larger population unit will also tend to expand the "scope of conflict" over development issues, meaning the range of interests and political pressures that are brought to bear.[9] Elected officials and city staff in large jurisdictions will tend to encounter different sorts of interest groups and political incentives than their counterparts in small communities, which in turn may change the policy choices that the local government makes. Whereas small-city policy makers tend to experience neighborhood-level pressures, those in large-population cities may be more politically insulated from existing residents' opposition to new housing. City hall in a big city is more distant—geographically and psychologically—from the average resident. A public official in a big city will tend to have a large number and variety of neighborhoods within her constituency, whereas a mayor or councilmember in a small municipality is responsible for much smaller, and often more homogeneous, areas.

In addition, numerous studies indicate that residents of larger jurisdictions tend to vote and engage in other forms of political participation at lower rates than residents of small jurisdictions.[10] This pattern suggests that in large cities, well-organized interest groups with a financial interest in promoting new housing, such as real estate developers, may be better able to capture local policy makers' attention while groups of neighborhood residents concerned about the possible negative effects of growth may tend to be less active.

Taken together, these factors can provide more maneuvering room in large cities for local politicians, who may wish to balance homevoters' concerns with broader goals for the city.[11] These other goals may include housing affordability, job creation, and what is often called a "good business climate," which can require sufficient housing supply in locations accessible to job sites. At election time, voters in large cities—like voters in states or in the nation as a whole—may hold their elected officials responsible for the economic fortunes of the city, such as its unemployment rate or affordability of rents. This possibility is particularly salient in the case of the mayor, whom voters likely presume (accurately or not) to be their city's chief executive.[12] The pressure on politicians in large cities to demonstrate healthy economic performance may induce them to be responsive to proposals for new housing projects.

In addition, businesses are more prevalent in large cities than in small ones, and businesses provide two types of resources that are important to local officials. First, businesses in large cities are a major source of local government revenues, in the form of taxes on property, sales, business income or payroll, and hotel stays. Second, the high cost of running for office in large cities means that it is usually essential for candidates to seek financial contributions. Among the various potential campaign donors in big cities, it is business interests—such as the chamber of commerce, major local firms, and real estate developers—that probably have the deepest pockets and among the strongest motives to fund local political campaigns and "bundle" contributions. In small cities, by contrast, progrowth businesses may be fewer in number and more sporadic or selective in their participation. These political factors can render elected officials in large cities more inclined to attend to the desires of businesses and somewhat less attuned to homeowners, in comparison to politicians in small cities.[13]

Another distinction between the ways that large and small communities approach potential new housing development relates to governmental capacity. Large municipalities are more likely to have the personnel necessary to plan and execute large-scale housing projects, including mixed-use developments that combine multifamily housing with office, retail, or other uses. These more complicated types of arrangements—which often require zoning changes and discretionary permits—frequently are the mechanisms by which major residential projects get built, particularly in already-developed parts of a region. In these so-called mature areas, such as the inner suburbs, large tracts of open land are rare or nonexistent, so new housing typically must be accommodated within the existing urban fabric rather than by extending the street grid into undeveloped areas. Getting infill housing approved and built can be a complicated public policy objective, and larger cities may have greater staff expertise to deal with the challenges.[14] The greater financial capabilities of large jurisdictions also may enhance their capacity to accommodate infill development.[15]

Race, Suburbanization, and the Proliferation of Bay Area Cities

If it is indeed the case in the Bay Area that the small population size of many jurisdictions in job-rich areas depresses the construction of multifamily housing, then a logical question to ask is: How did the Bay Area end up with so many small jurisdictions in areas accessible to job concentrations? This situation, it turns out, has deep historical roots. And importantly, considerations of race and racism feature prominently in this history.

The incorporation—that is, legal creation—of cities in the Bay Area did not occur gradually or evenly across the region's history (see Figure 1.1). Rather, there were surges in the creation of new cities during particular periods

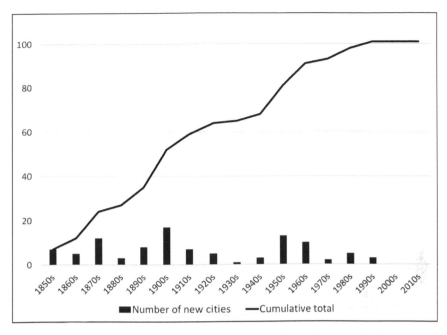

Figure 1.1   City Incorporations in the Nine Bay Area Counties, by Decade

when circumstances were advantageous for the founding of new jurisdictions. From the admission of California as a U.S. state in 1850 until late in that century, municipalities tended to form around an existing nucleus or commercial center. For example, San Francisco, San Jose, Oakland, Redwood City, and Vallejo, each of which had incorporated by 1870, had downtowns of varying sizes. But by the turn of the twentieth century, options for local service provision and revenue raising had expanded to make possible the incorporation of small and purely residential commuter suburbs, often with wealthy populations. For instance, Piedmont, Ross, and Hillsborough—all renowned in the region today as highly affluent bedroom communities—each came into existence between 1907 and 1910.

Incorporation enabled local governments to adopt zoning ordinances, which became widely used beginning in the interwar years of the 1920s and 1930s. Zoning gave local governments an opportunity to lock into place preferred land-use patterns—often by reserving areas for single-family detached housing, thus keeping apartments out.[16] Local real estate boards advocated for municipal zoning adoption in tandem with the use of private covenants to promote the goals of subdividers, who purchased large tracts of undeveloped land to be split into multiple lots for development and resale.

For real estate boards in the Bay Area, racial exclusion figured prominently among these goals.[17] The desire for racial separation among whites in the region was strongly connected to the fragmentation of local government. For instance, racial exclusion was one of the motivations for the separation of the elite suburb of Piedmont from the city of Oakland (which surrounds it) in 1907; after incorporation, intimidation and redlining were used to keep black residents out of Piedmont for decades, even as Oakland grew more racially diverse.[18] And during the post–World War II decades, according to a sophisticated study, Bay Area white residents who lived closer to neighborhoods that were experiencing an influx of African Americans from the South during the "Second Great Migration" were more likely to vote in favor of a statewide ballot measure that repealed fair-housing legislation.[19] Today, to be sure, the political geography of race and ethnicity in the Bay Area is more complex than in many other U.S. regions, given the presence of increasingly substantial populations of Asians and Latinos in addition to the black and white groups that are the focus of much literature on segregation. Nevertheless, in the Bay Area, as in many American metro regions, the restrictive land-use regulations adopted in the early twentieth century and beyond contribute to ongoing racial and ethnic segregation.[20]

The profusion of municipal incorporations in the early twentieth century was followed by a lull in the creation of new municipalities during the Great Depression and World War II. But thereafter, another burst of municipal incorporations occurred, with newly founded cities often taking full advantage of zoning and other types of land-use powers. Between 1948 and the passage of California's Proposition 13 property tax limitation in 1978 (which significantly restricted the property tax revenue available to support new cities), twenty-eight municipalities—more than a quarter of the Bay Area's total—were incorporated. Often located along the expanding freeway system, most were heavily oriented to single-family housing. This mid-twentieth-century period saw the creation of numerous municipalities on the Peninsula (south of San Francisco) and in the East Bay (Alameda and Contra Costa Counties). Many of these new localities would prove to be advantageously located with respect to job access—at least for those residents lucky enough to arrive on the scene before housing construction came to a close. Examples of such suburbs that today enjoy both prestige and proximity to employment include Los Altos, Campbell, and the previously described Lafayette.

The separation of these suburban municipalities from older cities, and their autonomous control over zoning, allowed many white suburbanites to avoid the increasing racial and ethnic diversity of the region in the postwar years, exacerbating long-standing inequities.[21] By the twenty-first century, as we discuss in Chapter 2, extreme increases in rents and home prices in the central part of the Bay Area had led to the out-migration of many black residents from the job-rich inner portions of the region to distant, underresourced suburbs that are far from employment centers. But meanwhile, according to a 2020 study, many older suburbs in the Bay Area with overwhelmingly single-family zoning, located near the region's biggest job centers, continued to enjoy unusually high incomes, home values, and school performance. Such municipalities' restrictive zoning renders housing costs so high that only the affluent can live there. As researchers from the University of California, Berkeley, noted, "These areas don't simply provide their own residents with these resources; they also hoard them from the rest of the Bay Area, especially people of color and people with low incomes."[22] These researchers identified thirteen cities most in need of zoning reform because of their overwhelmingly single-family zoning combined with proximity to jobs and economic opportunity. Twelve of the thirteen cities so designated had populations below forty thousand, consistent with the discussion above of the antiapartment tendencies of small cities.[23]

More than a century ago, the proliferation of municipalities in the region already was viewed as a problem. A planned state constitutional amendment to consolidate many Bay Area cities with San Francisco went to the statewide ballot in 1912 but was voted down in nearly every county. Other defeated plans in the pre–World War II years would have consolidated San Francisco with San Mateo County or combined multiple cities in Alameda County.[24] With the failure of these early attempts at regional reform, today's Bay Area has inherited the complex jurisdictional configurations that have accreted over time.[25] Self-governing suburbs, many of them small, control land use alongside key employment nodes and corridors.

In some parts of the region, moreover, as urban development expanded outward, it encountered a preexisting institutional architecture: municipalities that had incorporated decades earlier to meet the needs of outlying areas that—at the time of their founding—were small, rural towns well beyond commuting distance of the central Bay Area. Writing about the explosive post-1970 development of eastern Contra Costa County, Alex Schafran notes that "the Bay Area did not sprawl into an uninhabited desert in the postwar era, but rather grew into a regional skeleton of small industrial cities and old farm towns largely established by the end of the nineteenth century."[26] In that sense, the Bay Area—like its Southern California counterpart, the Los Angeles region—has been multicentered and multijurisdictional from the start. In the words of geographer James Vance, by the mid-nineteenth century, the Bay Area already was "characterized by an open extensive settlement pattern with

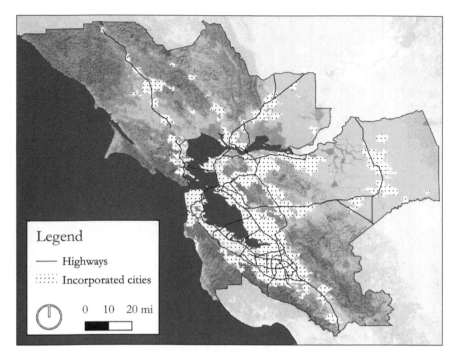

Figure 1.2 Highway Corridors and Developed Areas

a few major nuclei . . . stak[ing] out the limits of its ultimate site."[27] In the twentieth century, growth spread from these historic centers along transportation corridors, particularly in the era of massive highway building after World War II (see Figure 1.2). Still, a considerable share of the region's land area—particularly among its hills and along the Pacific coast—was preserved from development as protected open space.

The profusion of municipalities and nodes also meant that as the region grew, no single city was economically or politically dominant, unlike in many metropolitan areas. The multicentered nature of the region and its large number of governmental institutions likely has complicated the task of building coalitions for regionally beneficial outcomes, such as accommodating more housing and putting it in the right locations.[28]

A Plethora of Nonmunicipal Local Governments

The proliferation of small municipalities is just one manifestation—though a very important one—of the splintered and uncoordinated nature of public authority over land use and regional development. If we also take into account categories of local governments other than municipalities—counties, school districts, and special districts—there are nearly five hundred independent and separately constituted local governments in the Bay Area. Most of these governments hold some relevance for the interrelated challenges of land use, housing, and the services required to support communities.

The best adjective to describe the overall system of government across the Bay Area is *fragmented*. Indeed, calling it a "system" may give it too much credit, since that word, by its dictionary definition, implies an "organized scheme" or "a set of things working together." The 101 municipalities probably represent the most visible and familiar units of local government for most residents. They are "general-purpose" governments, in the parlance of local government specialists, providing a wide range of services in addition to land-use regulation. But any inventory of local governments also must account for the various roles of counties, school districts, and special districts, which we briefly describe here.

County governments—nine of them in the Bay Area—are, like cities, considered general-purpose governments. Unlike cities, however, counties function largely as agents of the state government, with the state imposing stricter constraints on their discretion than it places on cities. In this role, counties provide a considerable array of state-mandated social welfare and health services as well as criminal and civil justice functions, along with state-required tasks such as property assessment, election administration, and maintaining vital records. In terms of expenditures, these state-required activities are counties' primary functions. However, counties also establish zoning and subdivision requirements in unincorporated areas—that is, the portions of the county outside of city boundaries. In that sense, counties have a two-pronged role, serving as primary units of local government for residents who do not live in cities while also delivering state-required services countywide.

As new cities came into existence after World War II, usually near the suburban fringe, and as some existing cities expanded their boundaries through annexation, Bay Area counties were left with authority to regulate land use in a hodgepodge of disparate areas, neighborhoods, and subdivisions, along with (in some counties) considerable undeveloped areas of open space, agriculture, or public lands. Meanwhile, counties lack land-use authority within their incorporated cities. Thus, despite the much greater average geographic size of counties in comparison to municipalities, the ability of counties to implement an area-wide vision for balanced land use and transportation development is highly limited if not nonexistent.

Traditionally, many counties garnered a reputation as more permissive regulators than cities, although some counties in the region (most notably Marin) have pursued a slow-growth strategy. For developers, the relative lack of regulatory stringency by some county governments may make the prospect of building in unincorporated areas more attractive than it otherwise would be, even though unincorporated areas generally have poorer accessibility to jobs and services. The suppression of infill housing by inner and middle suburbs can increase the pace of development in unincorporated areas at the metropolitan fringe, thus contributing to outward sprawl.[29]

Superimposed on the landscape of cities and counties is an overlapping—and institutionally independent—layer of special-purpose government. This layer includes both school districts and special districts. Since neither type of government has zoning and subdivision powers, initially they may appear unrelated to the housing question. However, this is not the case.

There are 162 *public school districts* operating in the nine Bay Area counties.[30] School districts must wrestle with the effects of the land-use decisions made by cities (and, in unincorporated areas, by counties). Large-scale housing development in some areas necessitates new or expanded schools, even as other areas with established school facilities experience enrollment declines. Accordingly, school districts may be given advisory roles in the land-use regulatory process, providing input regarding the enrollment implications and effects on facilities of proposed housing developments. More important as an influence on the housing market, however, are reputations regarding the relative performance of school districts. High-quality school districts, as perceived by parents, can further escalate housing demand and housing prices within those districts. Differentials in school district reputations also can shape the set of choices that relocating families perceive as viable. In this manner, the geography of school district boundaries can funnel housing demand toward particular locations, thereby putting upward pressure on prices in some of the most exclusive parts of the Bay Area, including many of the small-sized suburbs in job-rich areas such as Lafayette.[31] Housing demand is amplified by high standardized test scores, and there has been a persistently high correlation between the affluence of school districts and their average test scores.[32]

Special districts are local governments, possessing varying degrees of autonomy, that exist to provide one specialized service or function—or in some cases a few interrelated functions—within a defined geographic area. Some special districts have the same boundaries as a city or a county; others overlap multiple jurisdictions or provide services in an area smaller than a city. Nationwide, special districts are by far the most numerous and fastest growing category of local government. Counting conservatively, there are 207 politically independent special districts operating in the nine Bay Area counties, plus many others that are subsidiary units of cities or counties.[33] Many special districts—such as those providing water and sanitary sewer lines—can help shape the path of development, and their decisions are not dictated by general-purpose governments.

More unusual, but important in the region's system of governance, is a category of special districts that cover a substantial portion of the metro area and provide region-shaping services like mass transit (e.g., BART, as well as the Golden Gate Bridge, Highway, and Transportation District), environmental regulation (the Bay Area Air Quality Management District), or other essential services and infrastructure (the East Bay Municipal Utilities District). With their responsibilities limited to a narrow range of services, however, and with constrained revenue-raising authority, even these regional special districts do not provide the capability for overseeing or coordinating the region's development patterns.

Implications of Fragmentation for the Politics of Housing

Units of government are founded to address specific problems for specific geographic areas at particular points in time. Once created, local governments typically do not disappear, even if they are no longer needed to address the particular problems that led to their creation. The result is an accretion of governing institutions and the fragmentation of authority over regional land use.

One set of social scientists celebrates local government fragmentation. Public choice theorists argue that having a large number of small local governments in a metro area forces the localities to compete to attract desired residents and businesses, thereby leading to greater efficiency and more responsiveness to residents' desires.[34] In the case of housing and urban development, however, we would argue that the public choice perspective somewhat misses the point. With regard to providing region-wide needs, such as allowing multifamily housing to be developed near jobs and transit, the profusion of municipalities frequently allows local governments to avoid responsibility, thereby creating an aggregate *inefficiency*. And the small scale of municipalities enables them to externalize many of the costs of their decisions (such as the traffic and greenhouse gas emissions generated due to a poor match between jobs and housing) onto the rest of the region. In this sense, fragmentation in land-use governance should be distinguished from fragmentation in the provision of routine local public services, such as libraries or trash collection, where competition may well lead to leaner, more customer-focused services. Finally, there is an equity cost associated with the fragmentation of land-use control: Residents' ability to exercise satisfactory choice depends heavily on their ability to afford the high price of purchasing housing in small, advantaged localities and school districts. Small and exclusive jurisdictions need not be responsive to or compete for lower-income residents of the region who cannot afford to live in that jurisdiction.

The profound complexity of governance structure in fragmented regions like the Bay Area can thwart residents' ability to hold public officials accountable for the region's most profound policy problems. The average resident is simultaneously governed by a city, a county, at least one school district, and multiple special districts. And that is merely while staying home. On the way to work, she will often cross numerous additional, invisible boundaries. To whom should this resident express her concerns about scarce and unaffordable housing, unequal public services and schools, or lack of convenient commuting alternatives? It is not clear which public officials in which local governments she should contact or whom she can hold responsible at the ballot box.

Residents *do* have clear points of access to the development process at the municipal level, where planning and zoning commissions and city councils conduct public hearings and undertake design reviews for proposed new construction, including housing developments. Recent political science research suggests that participation in municipal public hearings and planning meetings is heavily skewed toward homeowners and high-income residents, who often are vocally opposed to proposed new housing.[35] Although there are numerous opportunities for local residents to weigh in *locally*, residents seemingly have very limited input over the *regional* outcomes, such as scarce housing supply, that ensue from these thousands of local decisions. To be sure, the notable growth of the so-called YIMBY movement in California— "yes in my backyard" groups, which advocate for allowing more new housing—has changed the dynamics of participation over the past several years. Prohousing and renter-advocacy groups have been established, have gotten stronger, and now regularly speak out at local public meetings. Some YIMBY groups engage in litigation as well on behalf of proposed housing projects that local governments have denied.[36] Nevertheless, officials in the Bay Area's small municipalities surely remain cognizant that their reelection depends on pleasing existing residents, who are disproportionately homeowners. Young renters from out of town, dropping into a municipal public meeting to offer some critical comments, may not provoke quite the same level of responsiveness.

Altogether, then, fragmentation of local governance is not merely an academic concept. The political borders laid down across the Bay Area, usually many decades ago, have defined which interests are considered part of which communities—and delineate who is in the political majority in each place. Jurisdictional boundaries insulate local land-use decisions from broader regional scrutiny, privileging current residents' concerns about the possible side effects of proposed projects. The localistic nature of the debate over land use also serves to mute countervailing concerns at the regional level—such as the need for more housing supply. Boundaries shape residents' sense of which political issues are local and therefore amenable to influence and which issues are bigger than local and thus seemingly beyond their control. Boundaries also imbue residents with perceptions of shared legacies tied to their specific city (or school district). But as residents of the broader community known as the San Francisco Bay Area, they have no single institution, political process, or election in which to register their preferences for the region.[37]

Small-Scale Localism and the Elusive Quest for a Regional Approach to Housing

I n Chapter 1, we explained how the small scale of municipalities can restrain the production of new housing, leading to particular problems for a governmentally fragmented region like the Bay Area. If the smallness of a city dampens new construction, this effect should especially be evident for multifamily housing, since apartment and condominium buildings may seem especially "out of character" in localities where single-family neighborhoods dominate.

In this chapter, we first show empirically that the pattern of slower multifamily housing development in smaller communities does, in fact, characterize the Bay Area. We then discuss how housing developers adjust to this reality. Finally, we describe the decades-long efforts to create and strengthen region-wide governmental agencies that—at least in theory—might have the capacity and inclination to override localistic objections and push for more multifamily housing in job-rich parts of the region.

For both analytical and substantive reasons, our empirical focus is on multifamily housing rather than all housing. Our theoretical premise is that small jurisdictional size will tend to lead to local policies that dampen housing construction. Analytically, therefore, it is important to focus on housing outcomes that could be influenced by local government policy. In areas where demand for housing is strong, the primary constraint on *multifamily* housing tends to be local policies, such as zoning regulations that restrict density. By contrast, the main constraint on *single-family* housing in high-demand regions is more likely to be the limited availability of undeveloped land (e.g., farmland). The Bay Area is an older metro area where, unlike in some newer regions, vacant land is very limited, at least in the areas of the region proximate to job opportunities.

Our substantive reason for focusing on multifamily housing is that such housing provides the types of units most likely to be affordable and practical to develop in infill and transit-accessible locations. These are exactly the types of sites most appropriate for new housing in the job-rich parts of the San Francisco region. If mature metro areas like the Bay Area or the New York region are to build their way out of housing shortages sustainably, doing so will necessarily entail predominantly building multifamily housing on infill sites. The alternative—adding single-family housing in far outlying areas where job opportunities are mostly lacking—instead promises a future of sprawl and auto dependence.

Furthermore, in recent years multifamily housing has been the dominant type of housing developed in the Bay Area. For example, according to data from the Construction Industry Research Board, between 2011 and 2016, there were twice as many permits issued for new multifamily units (73,076) as for single-family units (36,068). For all these reasons, we analyze multifamily housing and the regulatory constraints to its development.

Empirical Evidence That Municipal Size Matters for Housing Development

We begin with some evidence from a generation ago to set the stage for a new analysis of much more recent data. A survey of local planning officials in 297 California municipalities, conducted by one of the present authors in 1998–1999, strongly supported the notion that larger suburbs tend to be friendlier to new housing development than smaller suburbs. In the survey, planners working for large-population suburbs (greater than fifty thousand residents) were twice as likely, in comparison to planners from suburbs smaller than that size, to report that their city's council majority "generally encourages" residential development. By contrast, planners from the smaller suburbs were roughly three times as likely as their counterparts in large suburbs to say that their city council's majority "occasionally slows" or "often proposes limitations" on residential development.[1]

Since the results from the survey of planners are more than two decades old, we sought to update our understanding of the relationship between jurisdictional size and housing production, with a focus on multifamily housing. We also wanted to move beyond survey-based perceptions to instead examine actual changes in housing over time. To that end, we analyze the change in the number of multifamily units between two iterations of the American

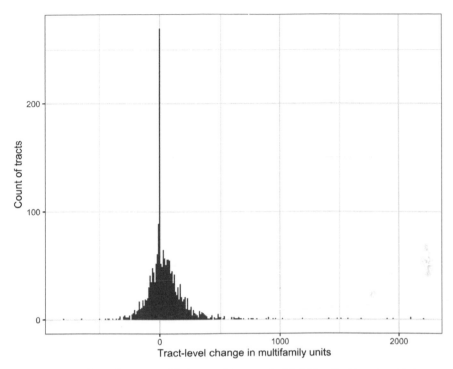

Figure 2.1 Distribution of Gains and Losses in Multifamily Housing Units across Census Tracts

Community Survey (ACS). We use *census tracts* as the geographic units within which housing change is measured. Census tracts generally approximate neighborhoods in size and are drawn by the U.S. Census Bureau to include 1,200 to 8,000 residents. The bureau conducts the ACS to collect estimates of demographic data at the census tract level, combining the estimates over multiyear periods to improve reliability. Here we analyze changes between the 2008–2012 ACS and the 2014–2018 ACS, a time span that approximately corresponds to the period of extended recovery from the Great Recession. The sample of California census tracts that we analyze, covering the state's major metropolitan areas, is described in the technical appendix.[2] During the study period, these tracts gained an estimated 105,353 multifamily housing units in buildings with at least five units, adding these to the 1.73 million units that existed at the beginning of the study period. As Figure 2.1 illustrates, however, more than 34 percent of the sampled tracts actually lost units (meaning more multifamily units were demolished than constructed), and 12 percent neither gained nor lost multifamily units.

Examining each tract's change in the number of multifamily units, we find that this number is positively correlated with the population size of the jurisdiction in which the tract is located. The magnitude of this correlation is very small, however, and the association is not statistically significant. Of course, the siting of multifamily housing clearly does not depend *only* on jurisdictional size. In order to account for other factors that could influence housing development in a census tract, we use regression analysis, which allows us to control for potentially confounding variables. Specifically, we control for the following characteristics of each tract:

- The number of *existing multifamily housing units*
- The *land area* of the tract, since larger tracts (all else being equal) should be able to accommodate more housing
- A measure of *accessibility to employment*, because we expect demand for housing to be higher in areas with better access to jobs
- The *percentage of housing that is owner occupied*, to take account of Fischel's homevoter hypothesis
- The *median age of housing units* already existing in the census tract, based on the expectation that tracts with older housing stock, all else equal, will tend to have less undeveloped land available to accommodate new buildings
- The percentage of existing housing units that are *vacant*, which may convey information about demand for housing in the tract
- *Average household size* (persons per household), because in areas with larger households, residents will generally demand fewer housing units, as compared to areas with smaller household sizes
- Measures of the *ethno-racial composition* of the census tract (percent black, Latino, and Asian), because these variables are of substantive interest, although we do not venture specific predictions about their correlation with multifamily housing development

By controlling for the tract's land area, its existing number of multifamily units, and the age of its existing housing stock, the model should account for the degree of "build-out" in the area—that is, how much space may or may not be available for new multifamily buildings.

In addition to these tract-level characteristics, we control for whether each tract is located within a municipality or within unincorporated county territory and whether the jurisdiction in question elects its legislature primarily from geographic districts or at large. The latter variable is included because recent research suggests that city councils elected by district are more likely to empower antigrowth interests, and thus reduce the issuance of housing permits, than councils where the legislators represent the entire jurisdiction.[3]

This analysis is detailed in the technical appendix. The results suggest that—holding constant the factors listed above—larger jurisdiction population size is indeed associated with a larger increase in multifamily housing. Specifically, a census tract in a jurisdiction with one hundred thousand inhabitants accommodated roughly forty-six more new multifamily units than a tract in a jurisdiction with thirty thousand inhabitants.[4] This estimate is particularly noteworthy, given that nearly half the tracts in our sample gained only five or fewer multifamily units, and the median tract added thirteen. The relationship between local population size and multifamily housing development is significantly stronger for localities with populations between one hundred thousand and five hundred thousand. Differences between, say, ten thousand and sixty thousand population do not show a significant statistical relationship to new multifamily units, but jurisdictions with hundreds of thousands of residents tend to accommodate considerably more new units per census tract than do jurisdictions with populations below one hundred thousand.

However, increased population is only associated with additional housing up to a point. In our sample of California cities and counties, once the jurisdiction's population exceeds one million, the tract-level association between population size and housing increase begins to fade. In a separate analysis of cities, counties, and townships in large urbanized areas nationwide, we similarly find that larger local government population size is associated with a greater increase in multifamily units at the census tract level, but only up to a jurisdictional population size of one million. The optimal jurisdictional population for enhanced multifamily housing production appears to be between 500,000 and 999,999.[5] Given that the Bay Area has only one city with a population over one million—San Jose, at 1.05 million—we conclude that increasing the average size of municipalities in the Bay Area, at least up to a point, would be likely to increase the amount of multifamily housing development.

Small Suburbs Dominate in Many Parts of the Bay Area Where Housing Belongs

The fact that small suburbs experience lower rates of new housing development is particularly relevant for the Bay Area because many parts of the region that are highly accessible to jobs have a profusion of low-population municipalities. To ascertain the proximity of employment in different communities, we use a measure based on the number of jobs within a forty-five-minute auto commute for residents of each city.[6] Figure 2.2 shows this measure of job accessibility for each city in the Bay Area's commuter shed.

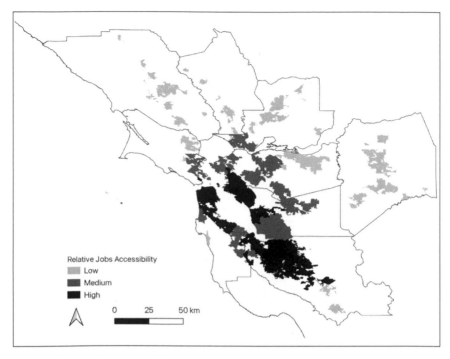

Figure 2.2   Job Accessibility in Bay Area Commuter Shed Municipalities

Aside from the job-rich central cities of San Francisco and Oakland, job access tends to be highest in much of the inner part of the East Bay region (i.e., the portions of Alameda and Contra Costa Counties closest to Oakland and San Francisco), as well in a corridor running south of San Francisco through the Peninsula and Silicon Valley. This corridor roughly approximates the route of U.S. Highway 101 and the Caltrain commuter rail line through San Mateo and Santa Clara Counties. In both of these job-rich suburban areas, many of the municipalities are relatively small suburbs where residential zoning patterns were established many decades ago, with large areas set aside for single-family detached housing. Of course, much land is also zoned for commercial, office, and institutional uses, consistent with the high job-access numbers for these areas.

To give another perspective, Table 2.1 lists the thirty most job-accessible municipalities in the Bay Area commuter shed. Municipalities with a population less than thirty thousand are shown in bold. Among the low-population cities that are highly proximate to employment are several conspicuously affluent enclaves, such as Atherton, Hillsborough, and Piedmont. However, some relatively modest small suburbs, such as El Cerrito and East Palo Alto,

TABLE 2.1 THE THIRTY MOST JOBS-PROXIMATE CITIES
IN THE BAY AREA COMMUTER SHED

City	Population (2010)	Jobs Accessibility Index	City	Population (2010)	Jobs Accessibility Index
1. **Emeryville**	10,080	3.11	16. Menlo Park	32,026	1.22
2. Oakland	390,724	2.13	17. Sunnyvale	140,081	1.15
3. San Francisco	805,235	2.04	18. San Mateo	97,207	1.13
4. **El Cerrito**	23,549	1.95	19. Campbell	39,349	1.00
5. **Atherton**	6,914	1.81	20. **Millbrae**	21,532	1.00
6. **Piedmont**	10,667	1.80	21. **Saratoga**	29,926	0.90
7. **Los Altos**	28,976	1.65	22. **Belmont**	25,835	0.89
8. Mountain View	74,066	1.64	23. **Brisbane**	4,282	0.87
9. Berkeley	112,580	1.47	24. **East Palo Alto**	28,155	0.82
10. **Burlingame**	28,806	1.46	25. Milpitas	66,790	0.80
11. Santa Clara	116,468	1.30	26. **Hillsborough**	10,825	0.79
12. Alameda	73,812	1.29	27. **Colma**	1,792	0.71
13. **Albany**	18,539	1.27	28. Hayward	144,186	0.69
14. San Leandro	84,950	1.24	29. **Los Gatos**	29,413	0.69
15. Palo Alto	64,403	1.22	30. San Bruno	41,114	0.68

Note: Cities with populations below 30,000 indicated in bold.

make the list as well. Not surprisingly, despite their humbler reputations, both cities had "typical home values" of more than $1 million as of February 2022, according to the real estate website Zillow.

Are these job-accessible communities experiencing a correspondingly high amount of housing development? Quite the contrary, in general. Figure 2.3 displays the percentage change in housing units for each city between the 2008–2012 ACS and the 2014–2018 ACS. To reiterate, the time span between these two installments of the ACS represents the period of steady economic growth from the nadir of the Great Recession well into the recovery—a time when demand for housing in the Bay Area rose steadily. But with a few exceptions (such as the formerly industrial small city of Emeryville, located along-side Oakland), the municipalities listed in Table 2.1 have among the lowest rates of housing increase during that period. In some cases, these job-proximate communities actually experienced a net *decrease* in residential units.

Other scholars of urban development, too, have noted that job-accessible, relatively close-in suburbs—where infill development is often politically difficult—frequently show anemic levels of housing production in high-cost metro areas.[7] Many of these small suburbs, despite enjoying excellent access to jobs, view themselves as "built out," having developed according to land-use plans and zoning maps created in a very different economic era fifty or more

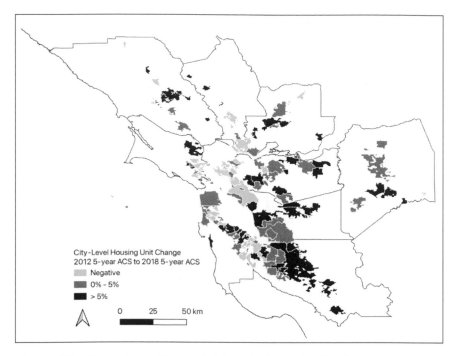

Figure 2.3 Percentage Change in Municipal Housing Stock

years ago. These areas represent a relative dead zone for new housing, or what economist Issi Romem refers to as the "dormant suburban interior."[8]

Central Cities Generally Do Better

By contrast, large central cities that are themselves job centers have made some progress—albeit halting and uneven—in accommodating multifamily infill housing. Although San Jose and San Francisco together constituted less than one-quarter of the Bay Area's population in 2010, between that year and 2018 about one-third of the region's new housing was built in those two cities, with more than 90 percent of these big-city units in multifamily projects.[9] The city of San Francisco is often lambasted by housing activists for the antidevelopment posture of some of its elected officials and neighborhood group leaders, but its percentage change in housing stock during our study period, while modest by national standards, exceeded that of nearly all its small suburban neighbors. Most of its new multifamily projects appeared in two close-in neighborhoods—South of Market, which has transitioned from an industrial and commercial zone to one with a significant residential presence, and the Mission, the traditional heart of the city's La-tino community, which is well served by transit. By contrast, lower-density neighborhoods in the more advantaged western part of the city saw little infill, with those neighborhoods' local legislators on the San Francisco Board of Supervisors (elected by district) often defending neighborhood groups that sought to limit development. Overall, however, notwithstanding its well-deserved reputation for lengthy, unpredictable reviews of residential propos-als, San Francisco performed significantly better in accommodating new housing than might be expected judging by the norm of the jurisdictions around it—a pattern indicative of how serious the underproduction of hous-ing is in the region.

The same better-than-average performance was true of San Jose, although like San Francisco it is falling behind its housing production goals, especially for below-market-rate units. In recent years, San Jose has waived development fees for high-rise residential projects near its downtown and suspended a re-quirement that apartment developers include ground-floor commercial space. This change in the city's policies may have contributed to a surge in multi-family construction, with more than 3,800 units being built in the down-town area (many near transit stations) from 2017 to 2021.[10]

But Oakland, the region's third-largest city, was a laggard in housing pro-duction during our study period. Market-rate housing production in Oak-land began to accelerate after 2016, as soaring rents in the region spread to the city and made the high cost of purchasing land and building there more remunerative for developers. Very little of the new housing produced was below market rate, however. Given the depth of subsidy that would be required to enable such housing, this should not be surprising. Instead, Oakland city policy prioritized acquiring existing housing and working with affordable housing nonprofits to designate the units as affordable, instituting income qualifications and rent limits.

Nevertheless, the central cities' poor progress on getting new affordable housing built has provided ammunition for some neighborhood groups and antigentrification activists, who argue that market-rate projects should be shelved until proportional amounts of affordable units are created. A resi-dent opposed to gentrification in the low-income neighborhood of West Oakland argued that if a mostly market-rate project is built on a currently vacant site adjacent to the area's BART station, "landlords and other people will take it as their cue to raise prices on everybody." Countering the anti-development perspective, other voices—such as regional YIMBY activists and local residents who want more investment in their long-depressed neigh-borhoods—speak out in favor of added market-rate units. "We're just surrounded by too many vacant lots," a West Oakland homeowner argued, in support of the same proposed apartment project. "Delaying projects like this one are keeping us from building the housing we need to support the growth of our city."[11] Thus, while housing development still presents a challenge in these larger central cities, their size and diversity of perspectives tends to produce a housing politics that is characterized by a closer balance between pro- and antihousing interests.

How Developers Adapt

Given the resistance of already-developed, so-called mature suburbs to entry-level, dense, or infill housing, what is a home builder to do? She could try to pay her way in—lawfully—by making concessions to the local government that might help counteract local opposition. For example, local governments can impose fees in order to collect up-front revenues that ostensibly will cover future costs of infrastructure for new housing.[12] Conflicts over such fees and exactions can be fraught, but some developers may prefer to simply pay such costs as a way to enable building in a desirable location. In high-demand housing market conditions, the cost of such exactions—estimated at $75,000 per multifamily unit in the East Bay city of Fremont in 2018, for example—can generally be passed along to residents of the newly built housing.[13] Neighborhood groups and city governments also may demand other types of concessions, including amenities like new parks that can be enjoyed by longtime as well as new residents. These demands may be particularly effective where there are voter approval requirements for certain types of land-use changes.[14]

Because builders can anticipate delays, heavier regulatory burdens, and higher development fees in the cities most proximate to jobs, they may seek instead to build on "greenfield" sites at the outer fringe of the region. In the Bay Area, the situation is even more pronounced, because the region's large amount of protected open space—while providing a valuable resource—has limited development at what might be called the "near fringe," pushing it to the "far fringe." These outlying housing developments, despite their considerable distance from job centers, often are built at surprisingly high densities, particularly in regions like the Bay Area where land costs are high. Unfortunately, the displacement of housing from job- and transit-rich areas to fringe locations often leads to lengthy commutes. Bay Area cities with rapid rates of residential growth—such as Antioch and Oakley in eastern Contra Costa County and Gilroy in southern Santa Clara County—generally are far from the region's main job centers and score low on our job-accessibility index. Such communities are essentially exporting workers, usually in single-occupant vehicles, to job-rich locales each workday. When the financial melt-down of 2008–2009 roiled the housing market, these peripheral residential communities—many of which have populations predominantly composed of ethnic and racial minorities—also bore the brunt of the foreclosure crisis.[15]

The pattern of interactions between builders and local governments often results in what William Lucy and David Phillips have called a "tyranny of easy development decisions," characterized by outward sprawl and a lack of infill.[16] In this scenario, developers choose easier, more predictable types of develop-ment, such as single-family subdivisions on greenfield sites at the fringe, while avoiding complicated, risky, or politically challenging options such as mixed-use infill in older suburbs. Facing a scarce supply of suitably zoned land for infill housing, residential developers often must request zoning variances or go through multiple rounds of reviews relating to design and other details of the project. These can be particularly intense processes in homevoter-domi-nant municipalities, where existing residents often perceive their community as already mature and complete. The complexity and local political unpopu-larity of infill projects in established suburbs can make the feasibility and cost of a development project more uncertain, deterring developers from even attempting to build in close-in communities. Delays inflate costs and reduce profits—especially since builders often depend on borrowed capital, where lengthier approval times mean paying more in interest.

The difficulty and added expense of a drawn-out review or variance pro-cess may prove too costly for small or less-experienced builders, driving them away from infill in favor of sites at the exurban fringe. This dynamic frequent-ly means that new housing gets pushed beyond the traditional nine counties of the Bay Area. Instead, subdivisions are built far to the east, in San Joaquin and Stanislaus Counties, which are part of California's inland agricultural heartland, the San Joaquin Valley.[17] Furthermore, lengthy discretionary re-views in the older parts of the region create more opportunities for perceived corruption, given the need for repeated interactions between local govern-ment officials and the would-be developers before permission to build is granted. Altogether, these factors may create additional antagonism between local residents and what they perceive to be "greedy" developers seeking "spe-cial treatment" or "favors" from local government.[18]

The Evolution of Regional Institutions: Are They Effective Counterweights to Localism?

Sensing how such localism has created gridlock for changes in regional pol-icy, some activists and policy makers long have touted strong metropolitan-level governmental institutions as an alternative. Despite the predominance of local government fragmentation described in Chapter 1, region-wide agencies certainly do exist in the Bay Area; actually, there are several. But the authority and inclinations of these regional agencies, and the manner in which their governing boards are chosen, do not lend themselves to effectively representing the perspective of the region's housing consumers. Nor do they represent *would-be* housing consumers—people priced out of housing in the region, who therefore live beyond the nine counties that traditionally define the Bay Area or do not have stable housing at all.

This judgment is not an indictment of the staff or board members of these region-wide entities, who—among many considerable accomplishments— bring important issues to the agenda for discussion and produce highly professional planning documents. Rather, as we describe in this section, none of the regional entities has sufficient visibility, authority, political legitimacy, or budgetary capacity to effectively guide the growth patterns of the region. Furthermore, until recently the compartmentalization of regional agencies by single-purpose function—with separately constituted regional entities for transportation, land-use planning, and air quality, among others—has hindered the ability of these agencies to offer a compelling alternative vision for the region's development.[19]

Regional institutions were born at varying times for varying purposes, but the period from approximately 1950 to 1980 set the tone for what these institutions would and would not be able to accomplish. Among the earliest larger-than-county entities in the region were the Bay Area Rapid Transit Commission (created in 1951), which ultimately evolved into the BART District (created by state legislation in 1957),[20] and the Bay Area Air Quality Management District (BAAQMD) in 1957. As their names imply, both BART and BAAQMD are formally special districts, devoted to their limited purposes: rail planning, construction, and operations in the case of BART and air quality in the case of BAAQMD. Those functions, of course, are strongly related to the land-use and transportation choices made by the region's many cities and counties, as the transit system and much of the air emissions are a function of where homes, workplaces, stores, and community institutions are situated. Neither district, however, has a great deal of leverage over local choices about what gets built where.

This is not to say that these districts have been passive. As it has expanded in recent decades, BART has promoted higher-density zoning and more transit-supportive land uses around its new and planned stations. It appears to be seeking to avoid its earlier pattern of surrounding suburban stations with park-and-ride lots, a pattern that may have actually increased sprawl by allowing some commuters the ability to live in distant (and lower-priced) suburbs while making the last legs of their commutes on rail. As noted in the Introduction, in 2018 the state of California passed legislation that drew upon the planning groundwork done earlier by BART, setting new standards for denser housing development within a half mile of BART stations. Yet ultimately, BART lacks the policy tools, the scope of control, and possibly the inclination to become a regional housing planner and developer. It must depend on the actions of others to realize the vision of transit density.

After the formation of BAAQMD and BART (and another regional special district, the Golden Gate Bridge District), the next major move forward in Bay Area regionalism was the state's creation of the San Francisco Bay Conservation and Development Commission (BCDC) in 1965. BCDC, initially a temporary state agency, was made permanent in 1969. BCDC's creation was spurred by public disgust over the ongoing conditions of the San Francisco Bay itself. Although the region is named after its most famous geographic feature, by the 1960s the Bay had shrunk considerably in size over the previous century due to filling, and water pollution was also an issue. Governed by an unwieldy twenty-seven-member commission including local government representatives and state appointees, BCDC avers that it "was not created to obviate or supersede the authority of cities, counties, and special districts that are located along the Bay and its shoreline" but rather to "view the Bay as an entire system, which is impossible for more narrowly focused governmental bodies."[21] Thus, while it has made real progress in repairing the Bay's ecosystem and improving public access to the waterfront, BCDC's charge is limited and is not focused on housing or broad regional governance.

More central to issues of housing and regional development is the Association of Bay Area Governments (ABAG). Founded in 1961, ABAG is a "council of governments"—essentially an intergovernmental forum, a regional version of the United Nations, representing local governments rather than nations. ABAG brings together delegates chosen by the nine counties and by the cities of each county to consider issues that cross local boundaries. Although ABAG was founded as a voluntary association of local governments, its accretion of important duties led virtually all cities and counties in the region to become members. Subsequently, it became a "joint-powers authority" of its member governments.[22]

In 1963, local governments agreed to increase ABAG's planning functions as a way to avoid the perceived threat of a new state law, the Regional Planning Act. This act would have required local governments in regions without cooperative regional planning entities to submit to newly authorized regional planning districts with taxing powers.[23] Instead, ABAG attempted to show off its planning talents, publishing the region's first comprehensive plan in 1970 and calling for one-third of the region's land to be devoted to open space. ABAG's work on other regional problems enabled it to expand into new functions, such as regional airport planning and a coastal planning effort that became a precedent for the California Coastal Commission.

Despite these early accomplishments, a staff member's embezzlement scandal during the same period probably doomed ABAG's chances at being designated as the region's transportation planning agency, which would have brought it substantial federal planning funds.[24] Instead, the state legislature created a separate body in 1971, the Metropolitan Transportation Commission (MTC), to take on that role. MTC serves as the region's metropolitan planning organization (MPO), an entity that federal law requires every metropolitan area to have in order to qualify for federal highway and transit funds. MPOs develop regional transportation plans that prioritize highway, transit, and other transportation projects for federal and state funding in order to meet specified criteria related to mitigating congestion and improving air quality, among other outcomes. In addition to federal and state funding, MTC has access to bridge tolls and HOT-lane (high-occupancy toll) funds to support its transportation investment program.

Nevertheless, state laws have repeatedly empowered *county* transportation agencies, which probably somewhat limits the leverage of MTC as a *region-wide* transportation agency that is tasked with setting regional priorities.[25] Although MTC coordinates with county transportation agencies, the county-level bodies have authority to finance projects through voter-approved county sales taxes and a share of state gasoline tax revenues. Two studies published in 2005 indicated that the county transportation authorities in the Bay Area "did not develop their expenditure plans based solely on" MTC's Regional Transportation Plan; rather, the regional plan was "simply a list of projects submitted by the [county congestion management agencies], with allocation of funds dictated by return-to-source" of the county sales tax money.[26]

In many U.S. metropolitan regions, the council of governments was assigned the MPO role, but in the Bay Area, that power was denied to the region's council, ABAG. For more than four decades, this separation of functions seriously limited the integration of housing and transportation planning in the region. It also limited the financial viability of ABAG as the regional land-use and housing planning organization, since the main sources of planning funds flowing to regions derive from federal transportation investment programs.[27]

Given its loss of the potential transportation function and the federal dollars that would have come with it, by the late 1970s, according to ABAG's then executive director, Revan Tranter, the association viewed itself as something of a "member-owned cooperative," with the members being the cities and counties that belonged to the organization. ABAG thus sought to prove itself capable of providing useful services to those local governments, such as bond issuance, training of local government personnel, and risk pooling for insurance purchases by cities. These service activities became a source of funds to ABAG as well as a carrot to draw in local governments and keep them engaged in discussions about regional responsibilities, such as housing, that they might have preferred to avoid.[28]

Under California housing law, ABAG oversees the state-required regional housing needs allocation (RHNA) process. To carry out RHNA, the California Department of Housing and Community Development generates a region-wide goal for housing production at various income levels. ABAG then allocates this target number of both market-rate and below-market-rate units to the 101 cities and nine counties. The local governments are then required to update the housing element of their general plans to demonstrate that they can accommodate enough residential development to meet their target. However, these housing allocations do not dictate what gets *built* in each community. Local governments, after all, are not housing developers per se. In order to address long-standing shortcomings in implementation, recent state legislation imposes stricter requirements for setting local housing targets and allows the California Department of Housing and Community Development greater influence to reject regional housing allocation plans. We discuss the RHNA process further in Chapter 3.

Past Proposals for a More Comprehensive Regional Agency

> Regional government is going to come, in time, because the problems are becoming more intensely regional. If it must come in time, we ought to start right now, in 1969.
>
> —San Francisco Mayor Joseph Alioto, September 14, 1968, quoted in Nathan and Scott, *Toward a Bay Area Regional Organization*

Regional government—that is, a *general-purpose government at the metropolitan scale*—did not come to the Bay Area in 1969 or any time since. But at various junctures it looked like a real possibility—including to many of the 750 residents and civic leaders who heard Mayor Alioto speak at a Berkeley conference entitled "Toward a Bay Area Regional Organization."[29] During several periods, regional and state legislative discussions seriously broached the notion of combining MTC and ABAG—or creating a new and more powerful agency that took on both their responsibilities. Already by 1967, a joint committee of the state legislature was deliberating about the forms a new metropolitan governing entity could take, in the wake of a failed proposal from

ABAG to "reconstitute" itself as a statutory agency with some implementation powers.[30]

In subsequent years, reformers from the business world, civic groups, the burgeoning environmental movement, and some elected officials pushed for a more integrated and powerful regional institution.[31] However, none of the many ambitious proposals for state legislation crossed the political finish line. John Knox, then a member of the California Assembly from Contra Costa County, sponsored several bills in the late 1960s and early 1970s to create a stronger regional agency. As Knox later recalled after retiring from the legislature:

> Regionalism as a word frightened a lot of local government officials. They said, "You're going to take over my city or my county. Or you're going to interfere with my jurisdiction, or what power I have. And I don't like it." And it was our job to convince them that we weren't trying to do that at all; we were trying to make them more effective.[32]

Although various minor reform bills passed, Knox's more comprehensive vision for a new Bay Area regional agency did not see the light of day. According to Revan Tranter, opposition came from both the political right—Sonoma County taxpayer organizations, for example ("the Tea Party of their day")—and from the left, such as "purists" who insisted on a directly elected regional government because they assumed that local politicians were in the pocket of sprawl-building developers.[33]

After a period when the topic lay fallow, in 1989 a "blue ribbon" coalition of civic, business, interest group, and political leaders, chaired by a former University of California, Berkeley, chancellor, initiated the Bay Vision 2020 campaign. Bay Vision 2020 had a specific institutional goal: to combine ABAG, MTC, and BAAQMD into one body. Once again, however, after much discussion around the region and at the state legislature, its recommendations were not enacted; the proposal passed the California Assembly but fell five votes shy in the state senate. Strikes against Bay Vision 2020 were that it lacked a clear mandate and did not identify a specific threat to be overcome while also excluding sitting local elected officials from its board.[34] In the recollection of one of Bay Vision's main proponents, "Ultimately there was so much inertia on the part of local government—especially the smaller cities that were afraid of being imposed upon by the bigger jurisdictions—that we couldn't get the legislation adopted that would cause a real merger."[35]

In the early 2000s, two bills authored by then state senator Tom Torlakson (SB 1243 of 2001 and SB 864 of 2002) sought to transfer ABAG's land-use responsibilities to MTC, thereby creating an entity that could integrate land-use and transportation planning. Neither bill was enacted, with SB 864 receiving letters of opposition from numerous cities and counties as well as ABAG itself.[36] Nevertheless, under these pressures ABAG and MTC convened a task force to consider structural changes in their sometimes-uneasy relationship. The task force evolved into a joint policy committee, which now calls itself the Bay Area Regional Collaborative (BARC) and also engages in coordination with BCDC. Its recent focus has been on regional strategies to address climate change, and it has also convened discussions of economic and racial justice in regional programs.

BARC was required to add representatives of BAAQMD by state legislation in 2004, which also directed the joint committee to report to the legislature by 2006 on "the feasibility of consolidating functions separately performed by ABAG and MTC."[37] Although a full merger did not occur, discussions were renewed a decade later, and the two agencies' formerly separate planning staffs—but not their governing boards—were swiftly, if somewhat controversially, combined in 2017. The staff consolidation notably included the executive director and other top management, who now jointly work for the MTC commissioners and the ABAG board. Proponents argued that the joint staff will create synergies for integrated planning of land use and transportation.[38]

Relatedly, in the early 2000s, another nongovernmental reform coalition sprung up from the ashes of Bay Vision 2020: the Bay Area Alliance for Sustainable Development. The Alliance's leadership, particularly a former state cabinet secretary and Contra Costa County supervisor named Sunne Wright McPeak, convinced ABAG, MTC, and BAAQMD to create a policy-based regional sustainability plan (a "smart growth" plan, in the parlance of that era). The plan's population and jobs projections were adopted by ABAG, which used them as inputs for RHNA and for MTC's regional transportation plan. The Joint Policy Committee (now BARC) attempted to create an implementation capability for the plan by adopting the concept of "priority development areas" (PDAs). PDAs were conceived as transit-rich locations that would become focal points of new development by awarding financial incentives to local governments that agreed to prioritize infill. Cities and counties nominate PDAs, which must be within a half mile of a transit station and be planned for future compact development ("focused growth") of housing and employment.[39] Money from MTC—which has spent more than $630 million toward infrastructure and planning in PDA areas—is the incentive for local governments to implement compact development, because some funding programs for housing and transportation have prioritized projects in PDAs.[40]

PDAs are a creative way to encourage local jurisdictions to consider how their transit-rich areas can contribute to regional housing goals. Nevertheless, it is notable that MTC's fact sheet reassures local jurisdictions that "establishing a PDA has no impact on a jurisdiction's authority over its zoning, development review, or other land use decision." Furthermore, regional plans "cannot supersede local land use authority" and do not "require any local action."[41] In other words, MTC, like ABAG, can provide encouragement and carrots to cities and counties but wields no real sticks—other than missing out on the carrots.

The Bay Area regional agencies' leadership on integrating transportation, land use, and housing planning and modeling set a precedent that the state legislature furthered in 2008 by passing Senate Bill 375. This legislation required transportation plans from all of California's metro regions to set goals for reducing greenhouse gas emissions and to measure progress toward attaining these goals.[42] In the Bay Area, the resulting Sustainable Communities Strategy later morphed into an effort called Plan Bay Area, with ABAG attempting to integrate the region's various functional plans with a view toward climate sustainability and housing production near transit.[43]

Thus, despite the "false start" of a proposed forced merger, former ABAG executive director Henry Gardner stated in 2011, "We got almost to the same place, and the two agencies are working extremely well together."[44] As the regional agencies emphasize in their current update of Plan Bay Area, however, implementing the sustainability plan "will not rest on ABAG's and MTC's shoulders alone, as many of the steps that will need to be taken will be outside the realm of the two agencies' responsibilities."[45] In short, cities and counties must *want* to participate in order for the plan's goals to be fulfilled.

In recent years, MTC also has convened a public/private strategy group called the Committee to House the Bay Area (informally called CASA), which issued its *CASA Compact* in 2019, with ABAG as one of the signatories.[46] The compact, which brought together major affordable housing providers as well as advocacy groups and local government officials, included a multipoint plan for state and local policy on affordable housing, including bond issuance and creation of a new regional entity to coordinate affordable housing funds. That regional agency, now known as the Bay Area Housing Finance Authority (BAHFA)—technically yet another special district—was created by a law signed by Governor Newsom in October 2019.[47] The law establishes the MTC commissioners as the governing board of the BAHFA, essentially giving the MTC a new responsibility, which should continue MTC's evolution into a multifunctional regional agency. The next key step for BAHFA will be to secure funding, a quest that was put on hold during the COVID-19 economic upheaval. BAHFA is authorized to issue bonds and seek to collect certain taxes on businesses (including a housing linkage fee generated by commercial construction) and then to allocate the funds to cities or counties for affordable housing or tenant protection programs.

Although at this time BAHFA's future effectiveness is very much unknown, the region has had considerable experience with its two most high-profile regional agencies—sixty years under ABAG and fifty under MTC. What lessons can be drawn from this long history that are relevant to the current debate over regional housing needs? First, many Bay Area leaders, in and outside of government, have recognized the need, and energetically made the case, for a regional entity more powerful and integrated than what has thus far existed. Second, the two main regional agencies, after a somewhat bumpy start, have increasingly found ways to work together productively, including sometimes innovative joint planning. But third, no matter how forward looking and well prepared ABAG's regional land-use plans have been, the capability to implement them remains lacking. As former BCDC executive director Joseph Bodovitz put it succinctly in 2003, "ABAG has long had a dedicated planning staff working on land use issues, but the association has no power to carry out its plans."[48] (This implementation shortfall is less true of MTC's transportation plans, which have a project orientation and considerable funding streams to make the road and transit improvements happen.)

In the area of land use, cities and counties retain final say over zoning, reviews of proposed projects, and the issuance of building permits—recent state legislation and court challenges notwithstanding. Even if ABAG and MTC were to be suddenly and completely merged tomorrow, perhaps even together with BAAQMD or BCDC, there is no reason to expect that the organizational shake-up would automatically lead to more housing being permitted in the region—not without some sort of regional power to review, and when needed to overturn, local governments' land-use decisions.

An Opportunity for a Reset?

I realize what I'm about to say is controversial. . . . I've heard several times the plight of the smaller cities. And I was wondering if it's something that ABAG could look at, that maybe, possibly, cities under 75,000 population need to look at possibly merging with a city next to them. . . . These are difficult times, and if the cities are not going to be able to survive, and go bankrupt, then maybe we need to look at other ways.

—Alameda County Supervisor Keith Haggerty, April 9, 2020, in ABAG Executive Board Select Comments

Perhaps this crisis with income inequality and COVID and racial injustice, . . . a recession, perhaps a depression all coming down at once, is an opportunity for a reset, for us to rethink how we govern ourselves and how we do land-use and transportation policy. You know, it's kind of crazy, we have something like 25 different transit agencies and 110 cities and counties in the Bay Area, all of which have different and independent authority and none of which are . . . truly accountable to any higher agency. And I just think if we were to start from scratch, we wouldn't do it that way. It's not a best practice; it's not how the great cities in the world have organized themselves. And if you look at the results, we have terrible traffic and horrible housing affordability. I don't think that anyone would argue that the system itself as it's currently designed—I wouldn't even say designed—as it's currently organized, is working. So perhaps this is an opportunity to have a broader conversation about how we create a regional system of governance that delivers better results.

—Former Lafayette city manager Steven Falk, June 3, 2020,
   in MTC, *Metro Talks: Equitable Housing*

Supervisor Haggerty's comments invoke municipal mergers as a possible response to local budgetary and service-provision challenges faced by small cities in the fiscal-emergency context of the COVID-19 pandemic. But city mergers—and, indeed, a fundamental reset of regional governance, as suggested in Steven Falk's quote—are worth considering for broader reasons having to do with the Bay Area's economic, social, and governmental viability. Over the long term, it is housing costs and availability that probably are the main threat to the region's economic sustainability and to the social mobility of its disadvantaged residents and its youth.

As currently constituted, however, the Bay Area's regional agencies are not up to the task of ensuring that housing is built where it is most needed. Historically, as Elisa Barbour notes, "the agencies with the strongest policy mandates tended to be narrowly focused, whereas those with broader policy purview tended to be organizationally weak."[49] Examples of the former type are BCDC, with its clear mission to preserve the Bay, and MTC, intended to prioritize and fund regional transportation projects. ABAG has the broadest mandate, given its daunting responsibilities of master planning for land use, allocating fair-share housing targets to localities, integrating land-use and environmental planning, providing insurance and bond services to local governments, and coordinating among the local governments and regional entities.

But while ABAG's purview is broad, its organizational structure is weak and its implementation powers minimal. Founded as a voluntary body, it often has been poorly funded and organizationally tenuous and has had to tread lightly among the home-rule-conscious cities and counties that constitute its membership. The recent absorption of ABAG's planning staff by MTC potentially represents an important change in trajectory, with a chance to more closely integrate regional land-use and housing projections with transportation investments. However, the governing boards of MTC and ABAG remain separate (though many local officials have served on both boards, sometimes simultaneously).[50] Furthermore, some voice concern that in the wake of the staff merger, MTC, with its much larger budget and its focus on winning federal transportation grants and getting projects built, might overwhelm the more comprehensive perspective traditionally upheld by ABAG.[51] In any event, the staff merger did nothing to reduce the firmly *local* control of zoning, land-use decisions, and discretionary review of housing proposals.

One essential actor in any potential reset of Bay Area governance that we have thus far mentioned only in passing is the State of California. Like all state governments, it has ultimate authority to create, eliminate, and reorganize its local governments, although the state constitution also grants a substantial degree of home rule to those cities and counties that have local charters. The state's authority to restructure local governance would apply as well to the state-created MTC and (in its joint-powers authority role) ABAG. State legislation adopted over the past several decades has significantly affected the obligations and prerogatives of regional entities and local governments alike—for example, in spelling out responsibilities for the RHNA process and in requiring a joint committee between four regional agencies. On a more fundamental level, the fiscal system that state law has imposed on local governments (including limitations on property tax increases and the awarding of a portion of sales tax revenues to the jurisdiction in which the sale occurs) has strongly shaped the incentives facing local governments as they make land-use decisions.[52]

By declaring the housing shortage as a matter of statewide concern, recent state legislation also has importantly asserted a right of the state to intervene in, or overrule, certain heretofore local land-use choices. Examples of such legislation include the Housing Accountability Act (significantly strengthened in 2017)[53] and the BART station-area housing law (AB 2923), as well as measures to expedite local housing approvals (SB 35) and authorize the California Department of Housing and Community Development to standardize the local housing planning process (SB 6).[54] Several of these laws could affect implementation of the California Environmental Quality Act, which has also shaped the opportunities and constraints faced by local governments considering projects. Significant in its absence—but still a theoretical possibility—is a state law to fully consolidate ABAG, MTC, and perhaps other regional bodies into something new and more powerful.

In short, the state is the potential wild-card player in Bay Area regional governance. Ambitious new legislation could potentially change the ground rules for local planning and housing development. Or, state lawmakers could rearrange the structure of local and regional government. In the next chapter, we provide a menu of possible governance reform options both at the state and regional level, with particular reference to addressing the region's housing dilemma.

Reshaping Governance Structure to Enhance Housing Opportunity

Six Options

W hen any system is broken, consideration of its repair or replacement is merited in order to avoid further damage. This maxim is no less true for a system of governance. However, any new proposal for reform entails uncertainties and potential pitfalls as well as advantages.[1] In this chapter, we provide a menu of possible options to restructure the governance of land use and housing development in the Bay Area. We examine a range of possible institutional and legislative changes, some relatively incremental and limited, others more thoroughgoing. The goal is not a mere "tidying up" of a complex system of government—an institutional reorganization for its own sake. Lest structural changes be compared to rearranging the deck chairs on the *Titanic*, we emphasize the potential effects of such changes on improving the supply and affordability of housing—particularly multifamily and infill units in job-accessible locations.

To be sure, our assessments rely heavily on educated guesswork. There have been few major structural reforms in large U.S. metropolitan areas in recent decades, and thus there is very limited empirical research to draw upon regarding the land-use effects of shifts in governing institutions. Our aim is to spur consideration of how a revised system of regional governance could further, rather than hinder, public values and priorities that are widely held in the Bay Area. Among these priorities are diverse residential opportunities, housing stability and affordability, broadly distributed and equitable economic prosperity, environmental sustainability, and inclusive public engagement in the issues facing the region.

In short, we ask how the Bay Area's system of land-use governance can be made more responsive to people's needs as "regional citizens," rather than responding primarily to defenders of small pieces of metropolitan turf. In the following we describe and assess six sets of potential changes to institutions and legislation. The reforms we consider include:

- Consolidating cities
- Reorganizing the existing regional agencies
- Creating a new, and perhaps directly elected, regional government
- Tightening state rules for municipal land use
- Creating a state or regional appeals board for housing proposals
- Altering the state-local fiscal system

For each proposal, we evaluate its potential to enhance housing opportunity while also considering its political and administrative feasibility and its potential impacts or disruptions to nonhousing-related city and county services, finances, or representation patterns. We then provide our summary evaluation of the six options.

Option One: Consolidate (Some) Existing Cities

Chapter 2 demonstrated empirically that there is a connection between the population size of a jurisdiction (generally a municipality, except in unincorporated areas) and the pace of recent multifamily development across census tracts. Census tracts located in jurisdictions of one hundred thousand or more residents accommodate more new multifamily units than tracts in small jurisdictions, even after accounting for a wide variety of potentially confounding factors. Judging by the statistical findings—both in our California sample and in a separate nationwide analysis, the optimal jurisdictional population size for receptivity to housing is between five hundred thousand and one million.[2]

Therefore, one seemingly straightforward option for reforming Bay Area governance to better accommodate housing would be to combine some of the region's existing, relatively small municipalities into larger cities that cover broader and more diverse geographic areas. *Municipal consolidation* is the formal name for the process by which neighboring cities combine, with a new, larger municipality created in their wake. Under California law, consolidation is the equivalent of a municipal merger, with one city (usually presumed to be the bigger and fiscally stronger city) taking over the reins of one or more neighboring cities, which then cease to exist as legal entities.[3]

Currently, the Bay Area has many relatively low-population cities that control land use in areas highly accessible to job concentrations. As Chapter 2 showed, housing production has been low in many of these communities. Thus, they might be especially appropriate candidates for consolidation. For example, small- to medium-sized cities in San Mateo and Santa Clara Counties, and suburbs (like Lafayette) along BART lines in Alameda and Contra Costa Counties, where the potential for infill housing is significant, are in many cases underperforming in accommodating new homes.

Merging small, inner- and middle-ring suburban municipalities into cities of hundreds of thousands, rather than tens of thousands, could help change the local political conversation regarding housing development. Larger jurisdiction size seems likely to limit (though certainly not quash) municipal governments' susceptibility to localistic objections to housing and instead may help raise the voices of other types of interests in the political debate, such as employers, housing advocates, and racial equity groups. Thus, the potential of this type of institutional shake-up to enhance housing production is potentially quite significant. One proviso, however, is that since a newly consolidated city is larger and more diverse than the smaller cities that are being combined, it would face political and legal pressure to elect its city council by district, rather than citywide. Our statistical model reported in Chapter 2 found some evidence, echoing prior studies, that district-election systems may be associated with lower housing production.[4] This tendency may detract from the otherwise housing-promoting aspects of consolidation.

After a consolidation, since the zoning of the predecessor cities is retained by the new city (per state law), one should anticipate that a merger will not yield any automatic or immediate increase in zoned capacity for housing. Presumably, however, receptivity to housing ultimately would improve compared to what the smaller cities would have allowed, due to the political differences between large and small cities described in Chapter 1. In any event, zoning and other land-use regulations are subject to revision over time. In large-scale cities, such regulatory changes as well as discretionary review processes are less likely to solely or overwhelmingly reflect the interests of homeowners living in the immediate vicinity of a proposed development.

Previously, we said that this reform is "seemingly straightforward"—*seemingly* because, in reality, municipal consolidation is far more complicated than just erasing some boundary lines on a map. Existing municipal governments are unlikely to give up their existence voluntarily or without a strong fight. As discussed in Chapter 1, the Bay Area's existing municipal boundary pattern is neither arbitrary nor imposed from above. Rather, cities in the region (as in other metropolitan areas) incorporated, generally long ago, for various reasons that seemed compelling to local residents at the time, reflecting a bottom-up politics of self-determination. Each Bay Area municipality—even the very small ones—is a going concern, well developed organizationally, with a significant body of existing local ordinances; contractual relationships with employees, vendors, and cooperating service providers; and in many cases a significant sense of local identity among residents.

Thus, large-scale consolidation of municipalities would be highly challenging politically, administratively, and socially. There is no deep vein of untapped support in the Bay Area for merging suburbs into a mega-suburb. This is the case even though experience shows that geographically very extensive municipalities composed mainly of suburban-style neighborhoods can successfully endure and thrive. Think of central cities that have heavily "suburban" characteristics, such as San Jose, San Diego, Orlando, or Houston. Or consider mega-suburbs such as Arlington (Texas), Aurora (Colorado), or Mesa (Arizona), each of which has a population topping 350,000 and includes considerable amounts of recently built housing. In the Bay Area, aside from the three traditional central cities (Oakland, San Francisco, and San Jose), only the city of Fremont tops 200,000 in population, although twelve other cities currently have 100,000 to 175,000 residents, a range just above the threshold that our statistical model estimates to be relatively more housing friendly.[5]

If not for historical decisions made long ago, this governmental pattern might well have become more common in various parts of the Bay Area. Had the evolution of local government proceeded differently, very large suburban municipalities would today be seen as "natural," in much the way residents view the merged city and county of San Francisco as second nature.[6] In the post–World War II period, however, cities in other states that added considerable new suburban territory to their boundaries almost invariably did so by annexation (the addition of unincorporated areas to a city) rather than through consolidation. Thus, the most recent significant municipal merger remains the famous New York consolidation of 1898 (bringing together Manhattan, Brooklyn, Queens, and Staten Island under one city government).[7] The Bay Area's long-standing multiplicity of local governments, with numerous economic hubs arising and forming their own governments by the end of the nineteenth century and smaller suburban communities quickly incorporating in the early twentieth, provided little real opportunity for massive annexations of the type common in other states. The exception was San Jose, near the southern edge of the Bay Area, which was once surrounded mainly by agricultural land. That city engaged heavily in annexation in the decades after World War II. Perhaps not surprisingly, San Jose is generally viewed as more housing friendly than its smaller Silicon Valley neighbors and (unusually for a central city) serves as something of a bedroom community to its job-heavy suburbs. Today there are few remaining opportunities for cities to annex large amounts of unincorporated territory in the parts of the Bay Area proximate to jobs centers.[8]

Given the slow evolution of the Bay Area's governance structure, introducing major municipal consolidations to the region in the current era would likely be highly disruptive to its politics and its provision of local public services. Indeed, large-scale merger of cities is probably among the most radical institutional shifts of the alternatives discussed in this chapter. Bodies of local law would need to be rewritten for a newly consolidated city, new tax rates would need to be set (with tax equity across the uniting cities potentially hamstrung by Proposition 13's restrictions on property tax increases), and provisions would need to be made for repayment of debt incurred by the predecessor municipalities. Employment relationships with city government workers would need to be renegotiated (the law specifies that any collective bargaining agreements and retiree benefits remain in effect);[9] organizational arrangements for police forces, fire departments, and other city agencies would need to be developed; and on and on. Presumably, many public workers from the eliminated cities would be hired on to similar positions in the new city, but the hurdles would be significant nonetheless.[10]

Reformers of past generations often asserted that cost savings would result from consolidations, arguing, for example, that only one police chief, fire chief, and city manager would need to be employed in a merged city, rather than several. However, academic perspectives and empirical scholarship on the topic are mixed and at times quite negative about the relative efficiency of large-scale municipalities.[11] For municipal services other than housing and land-use planning, competition between nearby local governments may have salutary effects: Such competition may restrain costs and better align public service offerings with residents' preferences, since relocating households and firms can choose among many different packages of taxes and services. Large cities may indeed only need one police chief or library director, but they often have layers of management hierarchy that are not present in the flatter organizations of small cities (e.g., assistant chiefs, precinct commanders, deputy directors). Consolidating two or more cities also could lead to cost increases because of an inclination to "level up" service provision and pay scales to those of the largest or most fiscally expansive city participating in the merger. Large cities may enjoy greater bureaucratic expertise (i.e., governing capacity) due to their large staff size and revenue base but also may suffer from greater organizational and political rigidity or complexity (sometimes given terms like *sclerosis* or *ungovernability*). Granted, large cities may enjoy some efficiencies in capital-intensive functions (e.g., sewer and water systems, flood control), and they may be able to take on more ambitious functions that small cities cannot easily deliver (e.g., large parks and recreation programs, airports). But these types of services can be made available even to small-scale suburbs through special-district governments, which can be scaled geographically to meet the needs of a multicity area, or sometimes through contracts with neighboring local governments.

Several American cities, mainly in the South—notably Nashville, India-napolis, and Louisville, as well as a handful of smaller cities—have enacted city-county consolidations during the past several decades. Unlike mergers that combine two or more cities, a city-county consolidation brings municipal and county functions together, generally in the countywide area although often exempting some smaller municipalities from the merger. In the Bay Area, San Francisco has more than 150 years of experience as a unified city-county, although its territory is far less extensive than that of the other counties in the region. Consolidating a city with a county is a complicated venture and, according to recent research, is no magic bullet for improvement of governance, although there may be some advantages for a city-county in having a unified economic development strategy.[12] County governments are primarily in the business of providing state-mandated social services and justice functions, a set of responsibilities quite different from the main tasks of municipalities. Funding and effectively managing the broad mix of both county and city services has been highly complex for consolidated city-counties like San Francisco and Philadelphia, and perspectives vary as to whether this arrangement is advisable. Regarding housing, there is little reason to suspect that a merged city-county would necessarily be more accommodating of residential construction than a large city resulting from municipal mergers. In any event, most of the Bay Area's eight counties (outside of San Francisco) are so large and territorially extensive as to probably make city-county consolidation a nonstarter. Moreover, three of them (Santa Clara, Alameda, and Contra Costa) have populations exceeding one million, which our empirical analysis in Chapter 2 suggests is a threshold beyond which jurisdictional size has diminishing returns for multifamily housing development.

For those who might seek it, what would be the necessary process for municipal consolidation? Under current California law, at least 5 percent of the registered voters in each city involved in a proposed consolidation would need to sign a petition in favor of the action. The proposal, including a detailed plan for the new city's form of government, service provision, and finances, would then need to be reviewed and approved by the county's Local Agency Formation Commission (LAFCO). (Municipal consolidations that cut across county boundaries do not appear to be possible in California.) Finally, an election would be held, requiring majority votes from *each* of the participating cities.[13] This is clearly a tall order. Voters in many cities might fear losing local identity and responsiveness after the consolidation, while their elected officials might fear a loss of power and office, given that electoral competition is likely to be greater in the consolidated city. To overcome such challenges, the state government could devise policies to incentivize consolidations, perhaps through fiscal aid, debt forgiveness, or other guarantees during the transition period of a newly merged city, or the state could set policies that disincentivize small communities from remaining separate, such as minimum population thresholds for certain state aid. At the extreme, since the state is legally superior to its localities, the California legislature presumably could enact legislation compelling a municipal consolidation, although the legal and political fallout for doing so would likely be immense.

All in all, city consolidation, while very likely a net positive for increasing the rate of housing construction in the Bay Area, is probably too jarring and complex of a change and is highly unlikely to be adopted. Consolidation does not seem to be narrowly tailored to address the region's main development dilemma—housing supply and sustainable land use—given the complications that mergers would entail for other important goals, such as efficient delivery of municipal services. The implications of consolidation for equitable representation would likely be mixed: Not only would small, affluent, predominantly white municipalities be absorbed into a larger unit, but potentially so would suburban communities where less affluent or nonwhite groups have attained significant sway in local politics. In any event, we foresee little realistic chance for creating mega-municipalities through large-scale consolidation in the Bay Area. However, if current fiscal challenges in some small communities continue, there may yet be enough pressure for some limited municipal mergers to proceed. Nevertheless, those seeking simpler and more feasible institutional reforms should read on.

Option Two: Reorganize or Merge the Existing Regional Institutions

In Chapter 2, we concluded that although the Bay Area does not lack for regional governmental institutions, it nevertheless is not regionally governed. One reform option, then, would be to rationalize the existing regional institutions with an eye toward more effectiveness in *implementing*, not merely in *devising*, regional plans for land use, housing, and transportation. This section addresses possible changes to existing regional agencies, while the subsequent section considers the possibility of creating a completely new regional governmental entity.

Multiple generations of reformers have sought to change the architecture of regional governance in the region, from the Save-the-Bay conservationists who fought to create BCDC in the 1960s through the legislative efforts in the 1990s and 2000s to merge ABAG, MTC, and in some proposals other agencies as well. Although some reformers seem bothered simply by the Bay Area's sheer number of regional institutions, we maintain that (as in the case of city consolidations) reducing the numbers of agencies for its own sake ought not to be the primary goal. Instead, we suggest focused consideration about which aspects of regional governance structure may most contribute to the problem of low housing production and lack of housing opportunity near jobs.

Four sets of problems of the existing regional agency arrangement stand out: lack of an integrated vision, inappropriate geographic or functional scope, inadequate capacity for implementation, and inadequate representation of the regional populace. Some of these potential problems might be ameliorated by a shake-up of existing regional institutions; others likely would not be. To highlight the potential and shortcomings of harnessing existing regional institutions, we briefly note how one such proposal—a full merger of ABAG and MTC, perhaps along with BCDC and BAAQMD—might be evaluated along each of these four dimensions.

Lack of an Integrated Vision?

Many metropolitan areas have a single regional planning agency responsible for both land-use planning and transportation funding allocations. For reasons described in Chapter 2, the California legislature split those functions in the Bay Area between ABAG (a council of governments engaging in long-range land-use planning, including fair-share housing allocations to cities and counties) and MTC (the federally designated metropolitan planning organization for transportation). This division placed land use (including housing) and transportation into two different entities, which critics argue leads to inadequate integration of transportation investment decisions with land-use planning. After failed attempts at organizational mergers in the 1970s, 1990s, and 2000s, ABAG and MTC began working together more productively in the twenty-first century, including such efforts as the Sustainable Communities Strategy, BARC, and the joint planning effort known as Plan Bay Area. In addition, in somewhat of a surprise, the boards of the two agencies voted in 2017 to merge the staffs of both units. However, the governing boards of the entities remain separate, although there frequently has been overlapping membership on the two boards.

At this point in time, it is unclear what additional integrative potential would arise from a full merger between these two agencies (plus BAAQMD and/or BCDC). Their now-unified staff already has the opportunity to combine its transportation and land-use expertise. Unifying the two governing boards as well might make board members more attentive to the intimate interplay of transportation investments, land use, and environmental planning, since the same group would be giving direction to staff and responding to the implications of staff-written plans in each of these areas. On the margins, this might lead to more housing-friendly decisions. For example, money for transportation improvements would be parceled out by the same board that evaluates housing allocations under the RHNA process, perhaps leading to a perspective that rewards local governments for performance. On the other hand, as noted previously, many other regions have long had single agencies that engage in both land-use and transportation planning. It is not obvious that regions with unified regional planning entities (such as the Southern California Association of Governments in the Los Angeles metropolis) have accomplished more or done a better job of integrating housing, land use, and transportation. The problem instead seems to lie elsewhere in the structure of regional governance.

Inappropriate Geographic or Functional Scope?

Do the regional agencies have control over the geographic areas and functions that they need to be effective? First, consider geographic scope. ABAG and MTC cover the entirety of the traditional nine-county Bay Area region, but an increasing share of the region's commuters reside outside these counties (mostly to the east, in the San Joaquin Valley).[14] The most recent (June 2020) RHNA allocation assigned to the Bay Area by the California Department of Housing and Community Development[15] does not require or ask the region to account for these in-commuters as part of the region's existing housing shortage, so in essence it appears that the superregional aspects of the Bay Area are being written off at both the state and regional level. While ABAG and MTC at times have coordinated with their regional planning counterparts in neighboring regions, these efforts have mostly been informal. Realistically, there is little chance of expanding the areal jurisdiction of either agency—or, for that matter, of a merged ABAG-MTC.

Regarding the functions in each agency's bailiwick, we have already noted the somewhat awkward division between planning for housing and land use (ABAG) and planning for transportation policy (MTC). Air-quality analysis for the region is currently hived off in BAAQMD, although under federal law MTC is also required to consider the air-quality implications of transportation trends and projects. BCDC's functional scope is limited to protection of the Bay, which includes authority over the issuance of permits for some land-use proposals that have implications for fill, restoration, or pollution of the Bay. In practice, therefore, BCDC has stronger implementation powers than most regional agencies, albeit with a geographic scope mainly limited to land adjacent to the Bay. Merging BCDC and BAAQMD with ABAG and MTC again creates some potential for considering the interplay of land use, transportation, and environmental quality. But some observers likely would worry about the risk of reducing the prominence of environmental concerns within a multifunctional regional agency. This potential marginalization might be seen as particularly problematic in the case of BCDC, which is widely considered to have been quite successful in its limited mission of improving the ecological health of the Bay—the region's most distinctive natural resource.

It is also worth considering the limited geographic and functional scope of the region's many mass transit districts. Notably, this category includes BART, which is governed by representatives elected from districts in three counties and extends its rail lines into two other counties but plays only a bit part in land-use decisions, namely around some of its stations. These transit agencies, which are special districts rather than regional planning entities, are first and foremost operational organizations: They must primarily concern themselves with the day-to-day operations of their rail and bus lines (and—in the case of the Golden Gate Bridge, Highway, and Transportation District—that iconic bridge as well). In general, analysts of regional organizations consider it wise to separate the operational aspects of transportation from the role of planning and coordinating regional transportation and prioritizing among capital funding projects. Such separation allows for greater objectivity by the regional agency.[16] The multiplicity of transit agencies has allowed for useful redundancies and overlaps in the region's transportation system, such as the ability to temporarily replace trains with buses when BART's Transbay Tube is under repair or allowing some bus riders to choose a ferry when bridge traffic is gridlocked.[17] Thus, merging the region's transit operators and handing the keys to MTC does not seem advisable.

Inadequate Capacity for Implementation?

A much more important limitation for the regional agencies than lack of operational responsibilities is a lack of implementation powers for area-wide land-use plans. This shortcoming pertains specifically to ABAG. By contrast, MTC, as the region's federally designated transportation planning agency, has ultimate say over the funding prioritization of major transportation projects, such as highway expansions and mass transit projects. In that sense, MTC can put its money where its mouth is. Or to be more precise, it can allocate federal and state transportation money as well as some regional funds such as bridge tolls, deciding which of the projects nominated by local sponsors will get funded and which will not. Like similar metropolitan planning organizations in other regions, MTC thus has some real capability to ensure that the projects built are congruent with the region's transportation plan.

ABAG, however, in designing long-range regional land-use plans and allocating housing targets to cities and counties under the RHNA process, has relatively little sway over the zoning and day-to-day land-use decisions of local governments. If ABAG were to conclude that its optimal regional plan would place tens of thousands of new apartment units in inner suburbs that are near job concentrations and transportation routes, it has no authority to rewrite local plans in those communities to make such apartment development possible. For the most part, its plan is merely a suggested vision for the localities, which make their own choices about land use within their boundaries.[18]

The concept of priority development areas adopted by ABAG and MTC in recent plans represents one creative way of enhancing the regional planning agencies' leverage over local land-use choices. PDAs provide additional transportation funds for local projects as a sweetener for localities that agree to upzone to higher densities around important transit lines; communities that choose not to make the zoning revisions necessary to comply with transit-oriented development do not qualify for this set of funds. The PDA concept shows the potential for productive linkages between land-use planning and transportation funding decisions and in that sense may support the case for enhanced coordination between ABAG and MTC. Even if fully implemented, however, PDAs seem like a modest effort in the overall context of regional land use, and the available evidence regarding a similar policy in Maryland suggests that PDAs may not be very effective.[19] Regardless of the merits of PDAs, however, it is important to note that a full merger of ABAG and MTC was unnecessary to pursue this policy, given that the two agencies implemented the PDA concept while remaining separate.

The broader point is that a merger or reorganization of regional agencies, in and of itself, does not solve the problem of inadequate implementation capability. ABAG, or any successor agency handling regional land-use planning, would need enhanced implementation powers in order to have a real chance to change the trajectory of local land-use regulation. One option would be for the state to enact a planning consistency law, requiring city and county land-use plans to demonstrate consistency with an officially adopted region-wide plan, such as Plan Bay Area. Other states, notably Maryland and New Jersey, have, at least at times, required consistency between local plans and a broader guide plan, although in those geographically small states, localities were tasked with achieving consistency with a statewide rather than metropolitan plan.

A consistency requirement represents a possible option for the Bay Area but would place ABAG—which, after all, is an association of local governments—into an awkward, perhaps untenable position as a potential supervisor or overseer of local consistency. In that regard, as we describe in Option Three, a completely new regional institution might be better equipped to handle such a role. Additionally, a planning consistency rule has the shortcoming of being largely a paper requirement. Local governments would continue to exercise discretionary review over actual proposals for new development, providing an opportunity to delay or reduce the size of multifamily projects, for example. In that sense, even under a consistency rule, the upper hand in implementation remains with the city or county, which casts final judgment on proposed residential projects (barring a lawsuit with a court order). Perhaps for this reason, there is a lack of evidence that consistency requirements in New Jersey or Maryland yielded increased housing. Rather, reduction of greenfield sprawl development and reinvigoration of older cities and town centers appeared to be the primary goals of the policy in those states.[20]

Inadequate Representation of the Regional Public?

A fourth potential critique of the Bay Area's existing architecture of regional institutions—and, we think, a compelling one—concerns its shortcomings for democratic representation. ABAG and MTC, and for that matter BCDC and BAAQMD, are governed by boards that are explicitly designed to represent municipalities and counties. For example, of the eighteen current voting members of the MTC board, sixteen are mayors, city councilmembers, or county supervisors chosen by their colleagues.[21] The other regional agencies use similar methods (in some cases set out in state statute) to constitute their governing boards. In the case of ABAG, that entity is by definition an association of local governments, and thus its board necessarily consists of representatives of its dues-paying members.[22]

This "delegate" or "constituent unit" approach has certain advantages: It presumably helps link the interests of city and county governments to the goals of the regional agencies and may secure more buy-in for regional programs from local elected officials. At the same time, however, it has serious disadvantages. It sends the message that the policy-making work of regional entities is properly the province of the *local governments*, rather than being an effort legitimized or empowered by the *people* of the region. Bay Area residents may feel a sense of citizenship or membership in their nation, state, county, and city, but (if they are aware of the regional institutions at all) they are only indirectly represented at the regional level. Regarding any grievances a voter might have regarding regional issues, as a *citizen of the region*, the resident has no electoral venue in which to express his or her grievance.[23] Observers may wonder whether regional board members are invested in the needs and responsibilities of the region if their selection to the board depends on the assent of other local elected officials who do not themselves serve on regional entities. Jake Mackenzie, a Rohnert Park councilmember and then MTC chair, mused in 2019, "There are certainly some elected officials in Sonoma County who feel that as chair of a regional governance board, I should have a very parochial attitude." Mackenzie's counterparts in that county were unhappy with his position in favor of communities being asked to accommodate more housing.[24]

In dealing with this shortcoming as well, a merger of regional entities would, in and of itself, not be a solution. Rather, the rules for choosing the governing board of the merged regional entity—and indeed, the very definition of what a regional governing agency is—would need to be rethought.[25] We take up this issue further in the next section.

Option Three: Create a Completely New Regional Institution, Perhaps Directly Elected

On a late summer day in the tumultuous year of 1968, more than seven hundred Bay Area residents and public officials packed into a University of California, Berkeley, auditorium for a remarkable daylong discussion about how the region's governance might be reformed.[26] Conference participants clearly felt the region was on the cusp of major institutional changes and debated a variety of topics concerning the responsibilities, powers, financing, and representational system of a possible regional government.[27]

For much of the twentieth century, proposals for metropolitan area-wide government were the holy grail for reform groups around the country concerned about the interdependencies, economic growth, and social equity of cities and suburbs. As Chapter 2 described, the ambitious proposals for Bay Area regional governance discussed in the late 1960s and early 1970s never came to fruition. Many other U.S. metro areas saw similar efforts (often during earlier time periods), nearly all of which also failed to be enacted.[28] In short, creating a regional government—that is, a more substantial institution than the current set of regional agencies, one with some real authority to implement its policy vision—always faces an uphill climb. The concept is unfamiliar to most Americans, to whom its potential benefits may seem vague and uncertain and its potential costs and shortcomings worrisome. Moreover, it inevitably arouses the opposition of those who have thrived under current arrangements, such as incumbent local officeholders in many jurisdictions and suburban homeowners fearful of change. For black, Latino, and

Asian leaders who have achieved a modicum of power in central cities or other diverse jurisdictions, an elected region-wide body may appear as a threat to undo any political gains the group has made within their municipality.[29]

Rather than sweeping away existing units of local government—which would basically amount to a superconsolidation, or what is sometimes called an amalgamation—advocates of regional governance in large, complex metropolitan areas typically envision a bi-level structure of government (or potentially trilevel, if counties are considered a distinct level).[30] Bi-level regionalism was indeed the preferred option of many Bay Area reformers in the late 1960s. Under this approach, the municipal governments would continue providing most local services, such as policing, street maintenance, and trash collection, avoiding the diseconomies of scale that we have noted as a shortcoming of consolidation. At the same time, an umbrella institution, the regional government, would be tasked with functions of regional consequence.

Although attractive as a concept, it is not obvious in practice how to clearly distinguish *local* policies from *regional* policies. Consider the ambiguities around such functions as airports, arterial roads, and cultural facilities, for example. However, the Bay Area's most important region-wide policy dilemmas surely include the accommodation and placement of housing, housing's proximity to employment, and its relationship to major transportation routes (both highways and transit). These are policy domains in which municipal- and county-level decision-making has not served the region well. Thus, it would be beside the point to create a regional level of government without assigning it at least partial responsibility for land-use decision-making. What we have in mind goes beyond writing regional plans, although at a minimum an effective regional government should be assigned the land-use and transportation planning responsibilities currently resting with ABAG and MTC. Additionally, however, it should be granted at least some so-called police powers (functions relating to public health, safety, and well-being), which are the source of the legal authority of cities and counties to regulate land use.

Bestowing some land-use powers on a regional agency does not imply that every building permit application needs to be debated and administered at the level of a jurisdiction covering 7.7 million people. Instead, the regional role in land use might focus on setting standards and requirements for city and county plans, focused on regional goals of housing opportunity, sustainable development, and transportation accessibility. Such standards might include, for example, minimum density thresholds for residentially zoned land or limits on the parking requirements that localities can impose on housing in zones where residential infill is needed. The regional government might even exert direct zoning powers in certain limited geographic areas that hold regional importance, such as in ecologically sensitive areas or at transit nodes where high-density, walkable, mixed-use development would benefit the region. In other respects, however, cities and counties might retain their customary planning, zoning, and permitting powers but be required to demonstrate consistency with the regional plan.

Aside from regional land use and transportation, what additional functions should a regional government assume? We do not have a definitive answer to that question, but criteria and provisions for the assumption of additional powers could be written into the enabling legislation for the regional entity. Fifty years ago, the California Governor's Commission on Metropolitan Area Problems advised that a multipurpose government be established in each of the state's metro regions, to be responsible not only for regional planning but also for at least one additional function, from a lengthy list the commission provided.[31] The expectation was that after the founding of its regional government, each region could continue to deliberate about which functions were properly regional versus local, while giving the regional government an opportunity to prove itself as meriting additional responsibilities. This type of open-ended approach may provide some advantages in flexibility.

Two of the nation's most famous regional governance entities have exhibited this pattern of receiving additional powers over time as they proved their capabilities. Founded in 1921, the Port Authority of New York and New Jersey, as its name implies, originated as a bistate organization empowered through an interstate compact to improve the port shipping facilities around New York Harbor. Over time the two states granted the Port Authority additional powers that came to include building and operating bridges and tunnels across the Hudson River; operating three regional airports, a major bus terminal, and a cross-state passenger rail line; and economic development activities.[32] However, while it remains one of the most well-known regional organizations in the United States, the Port Authority holds limited relevance for today's Bay Area and its housing crisis. Essentially a multifunction special district, the Port Authority is more involved in operating its facilities than in planning its region's development patterns, and it has no direct land-use authority except as a developer of its own real estate (e.g., at the airports and the former World Trade Center site in Manhattan). More fundamentally, the Port Authority (like many regional special districts) lacks a close connection to its region's citizens, as its governing board members are appointed by the two states' governors. Under this appointment system, the chance that short-term political gamesmanship may interfere in the longer-term mission of the agency became clear in the wake of the so-called Bridgegate scandal, associated with appointees of former New Jersey governor Chris Christie.[33]

A second prominent, but very different and arguably more relevant, example of a regional government is Portland's Metro. From modest beginnings, Metro has accumulated several important responsibilities across a three-county region covering the Oregon portion of the metro area encompassing Portland, Oregon, and Vancouver, Washington.[34] Metro began life in 1970 as the Metropolitan Service District (MSD), a special district that was given minor but somewhat open-ended responsibilities by the state legislature. In 1978, however, voters approved a ballot measure merging MSD with the region's existing council of governments—called the Columbia Region Association of Governments (CRAG)—which had held regional planning responsibilities for both land use and transportation (i.e., combining the roles that ABAG and MTC held in the Bay Area). The measure also established that MSD's governing board would be directly elected. Fortuitously, in the increasingly antigovernment era of the 1970s, the ballot proposition was titled "Reorganize MSD; Abolish CRAG," perhaps suggesting to voters a diminution, rather than empowerment, of regional agencies.

In any event, the merger saw MSD taking over the regional planning functions of CRAG, which included the then new responsibility under Oregon state law to designate an urban growth boundary for the three-county region. The agency's operational responsibilities, some of which predate the merger, include managing regional solid waste disposal and running the regional zoo, a convention center, and certain cultural facilities, as well as an extensive set of regional parks and open spaces.[35] In 1992, voters approved renaming the agency as Metro (already its nickname) and granted it a home-rule charter. More recently, Metro gained oversight power for a bond-funded affordable housing program of over $650 million, passed by the region's voters in 2018. Metro is large compared to most regional planning entities, in part because it holds several direct operational responsibilities. In 2019–2020 it counted about 1,600 employees and adopted a budget that foresaw spending $841 million, although the majority of the expenditures were devoted to special purposes and enterprise functions such as the affordable housing program, solid waste, the zoo, and debt service. Metro's more discretionary general fund budget was about $142 million, a large amount in comparison to the Bay Area's regional agencies.[36] Its largest continuous sources of funding derive from its enterprise revenues (particularly a "tipping fee" it levies on solid waste) and property taxes.[37]

Metro's most high-profile activity, however, remains its integrated, long-range land-use and transportation planning, which it undertakes in conjunction with Oregon's requirement for each region to designate and periodically reconsider an urban growth boundary. As part of this process, Metro has pushed for dense, walkable transit villages around some of the region's light-rail stations. It also has enforced the state's Metropolitan Housing Rule, whereby each municipality is required to zone for certain minimum housing densities and allow for multifamily and/or attached housing. In short, Metro gives continuing attention to regional housing needs and is granted considerable authority to review local residential zoning. Perspectives differ regarding how wisely Metro has balanced its responsibility to preserve rural land at the region's fringe with its responsibility to enable sufficient housing opportunity within the growth boundary. Nevertheless, it represents a rare, perhaps unique example of a visible regional governing entity that regularly debates an area-wide planning vision—one that combines land preservation with infill housing—and also possesses some tools necessary to carry out that vision.

Undoubtedly, one of the characteristics of Metro that has elevated the prominence of the Portland region's discussion of growth planning is the direct election of its governing board. Metro remains unique as the nation's only elected regional government, with six councilors elected by district and a council president and auditor each elected region wide. Having an elected council gives Metro a democratic legitimacy that unelected special districts or councils of government lack.[38] Moreover, the necessity of politicians to campaign for Metro offices on topics of region-wide importance (i.e., housing, transportation, and open space) means that the region regularly experiences political debate about regional issues and that regional policy attracts significant media coverage. In short, regional issues have a political home. By comparison, most board members of the Bay Area's regional agencies represent and speak for city and county governments. As noted in our discussion of Option Two, a regional board whose members are chosen on a "constituent unit" basis implies a theory of representation in which the regional agency answers to the cities and counties, rather than to the region's public.[39]

Thus, for regionalists in the Bay Area who seek to promote housing opportunity and transit-oriented development alongside continued efforts to control sprawl, Portland Metro represents an intriguing example from a neighboring state. Among the several commendable features that might be adapted to the Bay Area are Metro's integration of regional transportation and land-use planning in a single agency that has significant sources of revenue, its power to require local zoning and planning to be consistent with the regional plan, and especially its direct election of regional leaders. Some of the most important regulatory tools Metro has at its disposal, however—particularly the urban growth boundary and the Metropolitan Housing Rule—have been products of Oregon's elaborate state land-use control system. That state system is an element lacking in California. California Senate Bill 375 of 2008 (requiring quantified regional reductions in greenhouse gas emissions) arguably has begun to push California regions along a broadly similar path, albeit without a "stick" for the regional agencies to wield against unco-operative cities and counties.[40] Some argue that Metro's presence as an au-thoritative regional implementer of Oregon's land-use rules has rendered the state rules more effective in the Portland region than in other parts of Or-egon that lack regional governments.[41]

At the same time, it would be naive to expect that a clone of Portland Metro could be transplanted easily in the Bay Area. Metro evolved gradually over a considerable period of time, receiving additional authority and powers as it proved capable of its prior responsibilities. In that sense, the agency has been self-reinforcing. The Portland region is considerably smaller, govern-mentally less complex, and demographically less diverse than the Bay Area, with only a single dominant central city—all characteristics that probably eased Portland's path toward regionalism.[42] By comparison, designing an ef-fective, nimble, directly elected regional government for the Bay Area—a re-gion of 110 cities and counties, with a majority-minority population of nearly eight million people—seems a difficult balancing act indeed. Then, too, state law in Oregon has helped provide a regional land-use agenda for Metro and accompanying obligations for localities. The next section considers whether state legislation in California might be a quicker route than regional gov-ernment reform to unlocking the Bay Area's housing-development potential.

Option Four: Further Strengthen Existing Local Planning and Zoning Requirements under State Law

To date, California's attempts to address its housing crisis through state pol-icy have largely entailed legislative changes to existing planning and zoning requirements, coupled with additional funding for below-market-rate hous-ing. California has long maintained an elaborate RHNA process involving (a) setting numerical targets for housing production in each region, (b) allo-cating each region's targets to local governments, and (c) evaluating whether local governments take action to meet their allocated share of housing needs. This system could be effective if local governments generally engaged in good faith efforts to establish reasonable goals and implement those goals. It could also be effective if regional and/or state-level entities were empowered to com-pel local governments to accept and implement regional goals. Recent reforms have focused on increasing the efficacy of the RHNA system, although their impact on housing outcomes remains to be seen.

Although a comprehensive treatment of recent state law reforms is be-yond our scope here, a brief summary helps explain how these reforms could address the housing crisis and provides grounds for concern that the reforms might be insufficient. The California Department of Housing and Community Development is responsible for setting regional housing targets, in conjunction with councils of governments (such as ABAG in the Bay Area) and the California Department of Finance, which provides population projections. Under a 2018 reform, the targets should be based, in part, on the number of units needed to reduce the percentage of "cost burdened" households in the region (i.e., those spending over 30 percent of their income on housing) to the level that would prevail in a "healthy housing market" (i.e., one with a cost-burden rate no higher than the average rate in "comparable regions throughout the nation").[43] Councils of governments are responsible for allocating regional housing needs to cities and counties within the region. This allocation should account for the existing and projected levels of jobs and housing in each member jurisdiction, as well as "the opportunities and constraints to development of additional housing in each member jurisdiction."[44] Once the allocations are established, local governments must ensure that their housing plans can accommodate their allotted housing units and that their land-use regulations (such as zoning requirements) are consistent with their housing plans. Historically, the sanctions for local noncompliance have been weak to nonexistent, although recent reforms may improve compliance.[45]

This system can be effective only if each component functions as intended. If the regional target is too low, then local allocations will likely also be too low. Even if the regional target is appropriate, it may be allocated to member jurisdictions in ways that are unlikely to result in housing development. For example, in Southern California, the process—until recently—has allocated housing units to jurisdictions in the inland counties of Riverside and San Bernardino far in excess of actual demand while underallocating housing to job-rich coastal counties such as Los Angeles County and Orange County. Finally, even if the local allocations appropriately reflect demand for housing, local governments must change their land-use regulations in ways that actually facilitate denser infill development.

Although the recent reforms have had an important impact, they may nevertheless be insufficient to address the state's housing crisis. For example, on June 9, 2020, the California Department of Housing and Community Development made its final determination concerning the number of housing units that Bay Area jurisdictions should accommodate from June 2022 through December 2030.[46] That number—441,176—is substantially greater than the 187,990 units assigned to ABAG under the department's previous determination from 2012,[47] pointing to the impact of recent reforms. But it is likely insufficient to substantially ameliorate the status quo of high housing costs, overcrowding, and lengthy commutes in the Bay Area.[48]

Even if the regional and jurisdictional allocations are appropriate, they remain numbers on paper only. Motivated local governments may retain substantial power to avoid actually accommodating new housing. For example, recent state legislation allows accessory dwelling units (ADUs) on most single-family lots. An ADU is "a residential unit that can be added to a lot with an existing single family home."[49] Given the expanded potential for ADU development, close observers of California's housing politics expect that many local governments will claim that these potential units help fulfill their obligations to accommodate new housing development.[50] Because the vast majority of potential ADUs are unlikely to be built, such efforts—if successful—could largely vitiate the impact of the increased housing allocations resulting from recent legislation. In short, the complexity of the state's housing planning framework, coupled with the interdependency of each component of that framework, poses major challenges for achieving ambitious housing goals.

Moreover, increasing the stringency of local planning and zoning requirements does nothing to alter the underlying incentives of local governments, and it does not create new constituencies to push for change. By contrast, the creation of a state or regional appeals board for housing proposals, which we next discuss, could have more profound effects on prohousing constituencies.

Option Five: Create a State or Regional Appeals Board to Adjudicate Disputes about Housing Proposals

Several states, mostly in the Northeast, empower developers of undersupplied housing types, such as mixed-income multifamily housing, to challenge local restrictions on housing development. Some of these states, such as Massachusetts and New Jersey, share important features with California. Like California, both states have had strong job markets and high housing cost burdens. As in California, local governments in Massachusetts and New Jersey traditionally exercised extensive control over land-use regulation, and courts exhibited substantial deference to local decision-making. Moreover, just as in California, both states have adopted laws that oblige local governments to accommodate their "fair share" of certain kinds of housing. Unlike California, however, they allow a zoning override for developers proposing qualifying projects in municipalities that have not satisfied their fair-share requirements. Although these states' affordable housing appeals systems are not panaceas, they could be adapted to address several shortcomings of California's current approach.

The Massachusetts system, which the available evidence suggests is the most effective of these housing appeals regimes, could provide a starting point for California.[51] Massachusetts assigns a fair-share goal for below-market-rate housing units to each municipality based on year-round housing stock as of the most recent decennial census. Developers of qualifying projects that include below-market-rate units can request an expedited approvals process that waives local zoning requirements. For example, a developer could propose a multifamily housing project on a site zoned for nonresidential commercial uses or for single-family residential development. Municipalities that deny such projects are subject to an appeals process, unless 10 percent of their housing stock satisfies the fair-share criteria or they qualify for a limited safe harbor.[52] If a municipality does not satisfy these requirements and it denies a qualifying project or imposes conditions that render the project economically infeasible, then the developer can appeal to a state board. This board applies a standard that strongly favors the developer, and it can direct the local government to permit the project. Judicial appeals are allowed, but courts rarely overturn the board's decisions.

Five features of the Massachusetts system are particularly relevant for California. First, Massachusetts has a simple, bright-line rule to determine whether local governments have attained state housing goals. By contrast, California has an astonishingly complex fair-share system, RHNA, which requires individualized assessments for each jurisdiction. California's RHNA system both requires extensive technical expertise to assign housing allocations and invites elaborate efforts by motivated municipalities to game the system. Second, Massachusetts' comprehensive permit requirement enables developers to avoid reviews before multiple local boards. Recent reforms in California reduce some of these procedural hurdles,[53] but a comprehensive permit would go even further. Third, the availability of a zoning override would greatly expand options for developers in California—for example, by facilitating development on parcels currently zoned exclusively for commercial use where retail is no longer financially viable.[54] Fourth, expedited review of qualifying projects could significantly reduce developers' carrying costs, thereby making housing development more financially feasible. Recent reforms in California have made some strides in addressing this issue,[55] but more could be done. Fifth, Massachusetts' burden-shifting requirements further bolster developers' confidence that proposed projects can be built. Whereas Massachusetts municipalities can generally deny a project for any reason that is rationally related to a legitimate public purpose, if a project is eligible for the housing appeals system, then the municipality can disapprove it (or impose conditions that render it economically infeasible) *only* if the municipality can show that the proposed project would produce "a specific health or safety concern of sufficient gravity to outweigh the regional housing need."[56] These concerns do not include typical grounds for opposition, such as increased traffic congestion. As a result, such a standard would make it much more difficult for local governments in California to block housing projects.

The Massachusetts appeals regime has reinforced political constituencies that have, in turn, helped sustain the law. Developers who use the law include local builders, as well as national firms that specialize in subsidized housing or "building and managing rental housing in 'high barrier to entry' markets where there is pent-up demand."[57] Developers have proved to be an important lobbying force and have also provided financial support to oppose campaigns to repeal the law. Notably, the most recent large-scale campaign—a 2010 ballot measure that would have repealed the law—was rejected by over 58 percent of voters.[58] The resilience of the Massachusetts law suggests that the relatively minor intrusions of a limited zoning override may be palatable to a large majority of voters in a liberal-leaning state, such as California.

Parts of the Massachusetts experience could help inform the design of a similar system in California, although some modifications would also be beneficial. California should seriously consider several core components of the Massachusetts model: a bright-line fair-share rule, a zoning override, an expedited permitting process for qualifying projects, and the creation of an administrative body to hear appeals under a standard of review favoring housing.[59] But the design of each component should be tailored to effectively address California's housing crisis. For example, whereas Massachusetts' bright-line rule largely privileges development of below-market-rate housing, California might adopt a rule that would encourage both market-rate and below-market-rate development. An effective rule could rely on easily measured data (such as numbers of housing units) and a simple numerical threshold. For example, jurisdictions that do not increase their housing stock by a specified percentage (e.g., 15 percent over eight years) could be subject to the zoning override for multifamily and townhome projects. This system would facilitate the development of much needed market-rate "missing middle" housing,[60] but it could also encourage construction of below-market-rate housing by making each below-market-rate unit count for more than one market-rate unit.[61] In addition, given California's size and the heterogeneity of its metropolitan regions, it might be most effective to organize appeals boards at a regional level, rather than at the state level as is the case in Massachusetts.[62]

How feasible is a housing appeals regime for California? The history of the Massachusetts system suggests that—once enacted—such a regime can be very durable. But, to date, legislation including a zoning override has failed to pass in California. In the past two decades, California legislators have considered at least two bills directly modeled on the Massachusetts approach, but neither one passed.[63] Two other California bills, which would have preempted local low-density zoning in areas proximate to public transportation, also failed to pass the legislature.[64] Although the legislature's recent efforts to strengthen requirements for local planning and zoning do include some features of the Massachusetts regime, such as expedited permitting processes for qualifying projects, the fundamental solicitude for local zoning designations largely remains in place in California, with the notable exception of accessory dwelling units (discussed in the preceding section). However, although the Massachusetts regime has now endured for more than five decades, its adoption was the result of an idiosyncratic set of circumstances.[65] This fact suggests that housing advocates might be well advised to keep this option in focus, as shifting political circumstances can create unexpected opportunities for policy adoption.

Option Six: Reform the State-Local Fiscal System

How does California's system of local public finance incentivize or disincentivize housing development relative to other types of land use? How might alternative fiscal arrangements shift local officials' land-use incentives? The starting point for any discussion of local public finance in California is Proposition 13, the famous 1978 "tax revolt" ballot measure that constrained property taxation in the state. Proposition 13 limited the rate of property taxation to 1 percent of assessed value. It also decoupled assessed value from market value by rolling back assessed values to the 1975 level and capping the rate of increase in assessed value at the lesser of 2 percent or the rate of inflation. Under certain circumstances, including sale of the property, the assessed value returns to market rate.

Proposition 13 has had at least five consequences related to housing. First, in conjunction with Proposition 218, a 1996 ballot measure that imposed new requirements on general taxation and assessment levies, Proposition 13 led to a significant *decrease* in the incorporation of new cities in California as compared with other states.[66] This consequence of Propositions 13 and 218 may have *increased* housing development by increasing the average population size of existing jurisdictions; as shown in Chapter 2, less populous jurisdictions tend to be more restrictive of new housing. The remaining consequences of Proposition 13, however, likely hindered housing development and affordability. Its second consequence is that Proposition 13 encouraged the owners of vacant land to leave their property undeveloped due to the increase in assessed value that would result from development.[67] Third, and relatedly, Proposition 13 also created a strong disincentive for current homeowners to sell because they would incur a much higher tax burden upon moving.[68] Fourth, Proposition 13 increased local reliance on forms of revenue other than the property tax, such as sales taxes and hotel taxes, which encouraged local governments to prioritize certain kinds of commercial development over residential development. Fifth, and perhaps most significantly, Proposition 13 shifted far more responsibility for paying for the infrastructure and service costs of new residential development onto developers and home buyers.

This last consequence has affected the decisions of both developers and local officials. Prior to Proposition 13, new residential development would generally result in sufficient property tax revenue to fund the infrastructure improvements and local public services necessitated by new development. After Proposition 13, this ceased to be the case.[69] A variety of new financing mechanisms emerged, most of which shifted costs onto developers and home buyers. Among the most prominent of these mechanisms are exactions—local government requirements that developers pay fees or provide in-kind benefits (such as parks or infrastructure) as a condition of development.[70] Even if exactions are perfectly calibrated to mitigate the impacts of new housing, they can deter some development. That is because, in comparison to a regime where property taxes are sufficient to fund the infrastructure and services necessitated by new development, impact fees require developers to bear increased risks of absorbing the associated costs (rather than passing them on to home buyers) during periods of recession or when the demand for housing sags.[71]

Moreover, the regulatory practices that enable local governments to strike the relevant bargains with developers can further constrain housing development. In order to maximize the exactions they can extract, local governments have a strong incentive to establish very restrictive baseline zoning, which they can then loosen on an ad hoc basis in exchange for benefits.[72] Although both California law and the U.S. Constitution impose some limits on this practice, local governments nevertheless have substantial room to maneuver.[73] The resulting ad hoc negotiations create at least three impediments to housing development. First, in comparison to citywide rezoning processes, the case-by-case negotiation of zoning requirements empowers immediate neighbors to mobilize in opposition to a given project. Second, when each project requires a rezoning, developers must acquire extensive information about which interest groups must be appeased and what inducements will appease these groups. These high information costs can scuttle some projects. Third, bargaining over the myriad details associated with complex development projects can have high administrative costs for municipal governments.[74]

Although Proposition 13 has undoubtedly affected California's housing market, and has probably deterred some development, its reform may not be either necessary or sufficient to address California's housing crisis. This is perhaps fortuitous, because the enduring popularity of Proposition 13 among the state's voters limits the prospects for sweeping reform.[75] In any event, the majority of property tax payments go not to the municipal governments that regulate most urban land use but to other types of local governments, namely school districts, counties, and some special districts.[76] Thus, reform of the property tax system is not narrowly tailored toward inducing cities to permit more housing development; rather, its effects would reverberate through many other aspects of the state and local finance system. Although there are many compelling arguments for reforming or eliminating Proposition 13, it is so deeply woven into the fabric of California's public finance regime that it is impossible to predict the impacts of its elimination with any confidence. By contrast, reforming land-use regulation processes could address the problems described previously with less disruption.

Although Proposition 13's restrictions on local residential property tax rates probably ought to be taken as a given for the foreseeable future, there still may be options for fiscal reforms that could provide more incentives for local governments to accept increased housing development. For example, any change in the fiscal system under which the state shares or distributes an increased proportion of revenues to cities and counties on the basis of local population counts—or, better yet, counts of housing units—would improve, at least marginally, the perceived fiscal payoff of housing to localities. Of course, the details of such revenue formulas matter: If each new housing unit, on average, is projected to cost a city more in services than it will provide in revenues over a relevant time horizon, local governments still might prefer that the housing not be built.[77]

What if all future increments in revenue deriving from local sales taxes were placed in a regional tax pool and then redistributed to local governments on the basis of population growth or housing-unit growth? Currently, one cent of the tax that the state collects per dollar of sales is returned to the local government within which the sale occurs, giving cities an incentive to zone for retail land use, rather than housing.[78] If new sales tax revenues were pooled and shared with other localities in the region, we anticipate that localities would begin to view retail development with somewhat less favor in comparison to housing development.[79] Over time, this might lead to land being zoned for residential rather than retail development and ultimately to more housing being approved. As with changes to Proposition 13, however, such a reform probably would provoke fierce opposition from many local governments that are more comfortable with the current fiscal arrangements. In this case too, then, the political effort involved in enacting the reform seems disproportionately high relative to the (rather indirect) benefits of the reform for housing production.

Evaluating the Options

Table 3.1 succinctly summarizes our evaluations of the six reform options. Each option is considered along four criteria:

- Housing production potential
- Political feasibility
- Administrative feasibility
- Potential disruptiveness to existing local government functions

The last criterion is included because one would not want to pursue a reform to enhance housing production if the reform's side effects on the many other important tasks of cities and counties were too extreme. Though necessarily somewhat subjective, the evaluations in Table 3.1 provide our bottom-line judgment of the likely strengths and weaknesses of each proposal. We conclude that Option Five—the state or regional appeals board for housing proposals—would be the most advantageous reform to pursue at this time.

If one were to choose single-mindedly among these options based on their potential to overcome local resistance to residential development, the preferred approaches would include creating an elected region-wide government, creating an appeals board for denied housing proposals, or consolidating many of the region's small suburbs into cities with populations in the hundreds of thousands. Consolidation of cities (Option One), in particular, is the remedy that is probably most clearly implied by the statistical analysis in Chapter 2. However, city consolidations are a good example of how a one-dimensional frame of evaluation may lead to suboptimal reform strategies. Mega-suburban cities seem likely to make nobody happy politically, and the effects of very large city size on the efficiency of routine local services, such as policing and sanitation, are apt to be negative rather than positive. Moreover, the effects of city size on housing production probably would only take shape gradually over time, as the new cities got going and began to alter the regulation of land use.

If the Bay Area instead were to create a new structure of metropolitan government from scratch (Option Three), we would join many scholars of regional governance in recommending a directly elected regional "umbrella" agency while retaining the existing layer of city and county governments. Like Portland's Metro, an elected Bay Area regional government could bring the interrelated questions of transportation, sprawl, infill, and housing opportunity into the mainstream of political debate and media coverage. And the potential powers of such an agency to overrule or demand consistency from local plans and land-use decisions seem likely to reduce suburban home-owners' outsized political voice objecting to new housing. An *elected* region-al government also would enjoy considerable political legitimacy, probably making it more willing than existing regional agencies to stand its ground in holding local jurisdictions accountable to region-wide priorities. Estab-lishing direct election of a regional government with real power would be a meaningful way of enabling democratic participation in the public issues of the region. It also would function as a mechanism to bring regular public and media attention to issues like the need for infill housing to limit sprawl and long commutes.

That being said, the twenty-first-century Bay Area probably is long past the point of being able to create a system of regional government from scratch. Installing a new, powerful, elected body at the regional level in such a large, complex metropolitan area seems like a long shot. For many local politicians and some populist groups, a proposal for a big, directly elected institution would seem threatening enough to arouse immediate opposition. Moreover, the potential benefits of radical regional reform are uncertain enough that the tremendous political energy required to enact such a reform does not seem like a wise use of the limited energies of activists and sympathetic public of-ficials. In short, seeking a strong regional government in a large, 170-year-old metropolis may be an example of the best being the enemy of the good.

Perhaps for this reason, Option Two, the more incremental rationaliza-tion of existing regional agencies, has been the preferred approach of re-gional governance reformers in the Bay Area over the past fifty years or so. MTC and some of the other regional agencies already are creatures of state legislation, which makes these entities susceptible to periodic alteration, since only some additional state legislation would be required. Or so the theory goes. But despite the support of powerful interest groups, business associa-tions, and state legislators, several generations of reformers have been unable to accomplish a merger of regional agencies. This failure is indicative of how many hurdles are involved in even a modest restructuring of regional govern-ance. Reformers' dreams of a superagency blending the current MTC, ABAG, BAAQMD, and BCDC responsibilities seem, at this point, to have slipped away.

However, smaller advances along this front have occurred. The recent staff merger of MTC and ABAG, and those agencies' joint work on Plan Bay Area and funding incentives for transit-oriented development (in the form of PDAs), indicate that there is always some potential, albeit modest, for en-dogenous reforms to improve the integration of regional land-use and trans-portation planning. More recently, the state legislature's 2019 creation of the

TABLE 3.1 SUMMARY ASSESSMENT OF REFORM OPTIONS

	Housing Production Potential	Political Feasibility	Administrative Feasibility	Disruption to Existing Municipal and County Functions
1. Consolidate (Some) Existing Cities	Potentially high, at least over the long run, but only if the consolidated municipalities' populations are in the hundreds of thousands and if the successor city does not promise to lock in predecessor cities' existing zoning.	Low, although fiscal stress in small cities may incentivize some limited consolidations.	Low/medium, due to differences across cities in administrative arrangements, tax rates, service provision, and collective bargaining agreements.	Potentially high, and probably negative for the efficiency of routine services. Some efficiencies possible in capital-intensive functions.
2. Reorganize or Merge Existing Regional Institutions	Probably low, but potentially medium/high in the unlikely event that the postmerger regional agency is given power to implement regional land-use and housing plans (or if local consistency with a regional plan is strictly required).	Medium if simply reorganizing existing regional agencies but probably low if the land-use authority of the merged existing agency is substantially increased.	Medium/high. ABAG/MTC already share a staff and headquarters. The new Bay Area Housing Finance Agency (run by MTC) could incrementally gain powers and revenue.	Low, assuming the new agency is only granted authority over functions currently in the portfolio of existing regional agencies.
3. Create a Completely New Regional Institution, Perhaps Directly Elected	Probably medium/high, but depends on authority granted to the new agency. It could supplant some local land-use decision-making or have new consistency requirements or veto powers over local decisions.	Probably low, based on past experience with major proposed regional reforms, but prospects could improve with skilled framing of a new agency as a democratically controlled means to address the housing crisis.	Medium. A new agency would need to be created and staffed from scratch, but skilled staff could be recruited from the existing regional agencies, especially if their powers were transferred to the new agency.	Depends on powers granted to the new agency and specificity of the statute. Disruptions would be greater if direct service and operating responsibilities were granted to the new regional agency.

	Housing Production Potential	Political Feasibility	Administrative Feasibility	Disruption to Existing Municipal and County Functions
4. Further Strengthen Existing Local Planning and Zoning Requirements under State Law	**Low/medium**, without further changes. Can ease some bottlenecks for housing proposals but does not create new constituencies for change or empower existing constituencies.	**Medium/high**, as demonstrated by the success of such legislation in recent years.	**Low under the current framework**, as the California Department of Housing and Community Development has limited capacity to oversee local actions, and the capacity of ABAG to impose unwanted RHNA allocations is weak.	**Low/medium**, because land use regulation is already a central activity of local government.
5. Create a State or Regional Appeals Board to Adjudicate Disputes about Housing Proposals	**Medium/high**, due to reconfiguration of powers and developers' incentives to monitor and challenge local regulatory practices.	**Medium**. Although past bills to create an appeals board failed in California and developers are politically unpopular, other states' experience suggests such a law can be adopted and may prove resilient.	**Low to high**. Such regimes can be associated with extremely cumbersome (e.g., New Jersey) or relatively streamlined (e.g., Massachusetts) administrative rules.	**Low/medium**, because land-use regulation is already a central activity of local government.
6. Reform the State-Local Fiscal System	Difficult to predict, but probably **low** in the near term, **medium** over the long term.	**Very low** for major reform of Proposition 13 as applied to residences, **low** for redistributing new sales tax revenues on the basis of population growth, **medium** for new state-shared revenues distributed to localities based on housing-unit increase.	**Low**, due to the complex, interconnected system of state, city, county, and school financing that has evolved since Proposition 13.	Probably **medium**, in the near term, due to difficulties in projecting budgetary effects, which might vary considerably across localities and school districts.

Bay Area Housing Finance Authority—to be run by MTC, wearing a different hat—is an intriguing wild card. Though its initial work was halted by the
COVID-19 crisis, BAHFA may yet gain the power and revenue base to significantly enhance housing production (and preserve existing tenant protections), although probably only in the subset of cities and counties that are
truly interested in adding or protecting below-market-rate housing.

Overall, however, the lessons of a half century of experience with ABAG's
and MTC's lack of power or inclination to overrule or supersede antihousing
decisions by local governments are not encouraging. This history suggests that
voluntaristic regionalism—the idea that instituting a regional policy should
depend upon the voluntary willingness of local governments to implement
that policy—probably will never be an effective path toward maximizing
housing opportunity in the Bay Area. Scholars have long observed that the
political feasibility of metropolitan governance reforms varies inversely with
the degree of interference the reforms imply for the lifestyle choices of affluent residents.[80] Past experience also suggests that regionalism through constituent-unit representation of cities and counties is a recipe for reinforcing
parochial local government perspectives. That is, having municipal and county officials choose regional representatives for their jurisdictions entails a
mode of representation in which regional agencies answer to the local governments, rather than to the region's public.

Options Four, Five, and Six depend mainly on state government action.
Option Four would continue the recent path of legislation to tighten the RHNA
process or restrict the discretion of local governments regarding certain types
of housing proposals. There are early indications that some new housing has
indeed been enabled by these types of legislative changes, and more could
likely be accomplished along these lines. But Option Four does not fundamentally change the incentives of local governments to want or accept housing.
Nor (unlike Options One, Three, and Five) does it provide a new institutional "home" around which prohousing interests might coalesce and for-
mulate supportive policies. Instead, Option Four's tenor is mainly geared
at increasing adversarial oversight of local land-use decisions by state government.

Option Six would promote fiscal reform, attempting to change local government incentives so as to make housing more remunerative for local trea-
suries. But although Proposition 13's property tax restrictions are a frequent
target of blame for the state's housing crisis (and for many other problems),
our perspective is that reforming the property tax system would be only an
indirect way to accelerate housing production. Changes in the means of financing local governments might well alter the comparative attractiveness
to cities of housing, retail, and other types of land uses, but such effects seem

highly dependent on the exact funding formula used and would take time to work their way through the system. In any event, reform of state-local fiscal arrangements would prove extremely difficult politically. Despite the dismay often directed at Proposition 13, it is clear that low-density, exclusionary zoning came into existence well before 1978, when that ballot measure passed. Moreover, exclusionary communities with low-density zoning certainly exist in states that lack strict property tax limitations. In short, fiscal reform might be a good idea for a variety of reasons, but aside from its inherent political difficulty, it seems neither necessary nor sufficient to boost housing production in the near term.

That leaves Option Five, the appeals board for housing proposals that have been denied by cities or counties. At first blush, it appears a modest change in comparison to several of the other options. But it has several advantages. The appeals-board concept has a track record in other states, and empirical research indicates that (especially in Massachusetts) it has significant positive effects on housing production. Unlike Options Four or Six, it creates a new institutional venue, an outlet for prohousing interests that are blocked or frustrated by local decisions. In that sense, it becomes a method for overcoming an age-old problem in politics, the difficulty in enacting changes whose benefits are broad (in this case, enhanced housing opportunity across the region) but whose costs are perceived to narrowly affect a specific group (in this case, homeowners in a single community).[81]

Unlike more grandiose proposals for regional government, an appeals board can be designed as a relatively simple, low-cost institution, with a clearly delimited responsibility, that could operate with dispatch. A bright-line standard can be specified that would indicate both to local governments and to housing developers which localities would be subject to having their denials appealed and what types of housing proposals would be eligible for appeal. In the short run, appeals would be heard, many presumably would be decided so as to overrule the local government's denial, and housing projects would receive their permits and be built. Over the longer term, the very presence and threat of the appeals board would reduce the bargaining power of local antihousing interests. Wary of being overruled, local governments likely would be less obstructive of proposals and more willing to entertain home builders' proposals, perhaps embracing more timely and predictable forms of negotiation to allay neighbors' concerns. Local officials also would come to realize that the way to avoid the appeals board's scrutiny would be to meet their bright-line target for provision of housing. If threatened with elimination, the appeals board is likely to have vocal defenders: nonprofit builders of affordable housing, commercial developers, prohousing activists, regional civic and business organizations, environmental groups in favor of compact development, sympathetic state legislators, and even local officials who hail from communities that *have* met their bright-line target and resent the evasion of housing responsibilities by more advantaged jurisdictions.

For these reasons, Option Five seems workable and sustainable. Less dramatic and less institutionally disruptive than some of the other options, it promises a high ratio of benefit to political and administrative difficulty, particularly over the short to medium term. Over the longer term, reformers certainly could continue to pursue additional options. The existence of an appeals board would not preclude these other reform options, and their prospects might even be enhanced by the measurable success of such a board. Thus, over time, Option Five might productively be combined with additional approaches, such as a reorganization of regional institutions, the consolidation of some municipalities, reform of the state-local fiscal system, or even direct regional elections—either of the regional appeals board itself or, more likely, of a regional government that might appoint appeals-board members.

Conclusion

Lessons of Housing Politics and Regional Reform

W hen it comes to housing, the experience of the San Francisco Bay
Area unfortunately offers a cautionary tale to other metropolitan
areas. Nevertheless, that is not to say that other regions cannot
learn from this case. The need to focus on governance as part of the housing
challenge is a lesson that is applicable beyond the Bay Area. Leaving a solution up to individual cities—whether large central cities like San Francisco
or San Jose or modest-sized suburbs like Lafayette—is unlikely to lead to
increased housing supply. Rather, regional-level action—with the active support of the state government—is needed to wrestle with a problem as big as
housing.

We have argued that the structure of government in the Bay Area—and,
in particular, control of land use by small-population jurisdictions in job-
rich areas—severely compromises the region's ability to respond effectively
to its housing shortage. Under its current governmental system, implementing
an effective regional strategy to increase housing opportunity would basically necessitate convincing all or most of the Bay Area's 101 cities and nine
counties to individually make the regulatory changes, land-use decisions,
and financial investments needed to produce more housing opportunities.
But these local governments are elected by local, not regional, voters and
thus tend to respond to the concerns raised by their existing residents, particularly homeowners. Obstruction or indecision from any substantial portion of those local governments, particularly those located near the region's

job centers and in transit-rich areas, would doom a regional housing effort. That is basically what has happened in recent decades, as advantageously located communities have failed to enable significant residential production. Regional housing supply has slipped further and further behind needs while rents (except during the early part of the COVID-19 pandemic), home prices, and homelessness have soared.

One important—probably essential—reform that is needed to help ameliorate this set of problems involves change to the structure of governance in the region. Simply put, sufficient housing cannot be produced without unlocking the development potential of underutilized sites in the job-rich areas of the region. And an important way to accomplish that unlocking is to institutionally empower a force that counteracts the prevailing small-scale localism of the Bay Area's current system of government. A regional governmental voice is needed that accommodates productive, equitable changes in the Bay Area's growth patterns, furthering the region-wide interest in sustainable, well-located development. An entity with real authority is needed to balance, question, and sometimes veto the many local voices that prefer stasis and comfort the already comfortable.

At present, local government in the Bay Area, as in most large metropolitan regions in the United States, is highly fragmented. This is particularly the case in the inner and mid-suburbs, which tend to be close to major employment centers and where the potential for productive infill development is high. A fragmented system of land-use control has little leverage to ensure that new housing gets developed close to locations with expanding job opportunities. In such a system, nobody can insist that new commercial growth around freeway exits must not come at the expense of existing centers or that high-capacity transit corridors must allow large amounts of entry-level multifamily housing within walking distance. Nor can a highly localized land-use decision-making process do much to remediate the wide disparities in tax base, economic resources, or social conditions that arise across jurisdictions. Instead of building housing in high-opportunity communities such as Lafayette, developers often follow a path of least resistance, constructing new housing at the region's fringe or hours away in the San Joaquin Valley. As a result, commutes get longer, highways become more overloaded, and productive agricultural land turns into tract housing, even as some coastal communities with good infrastructure capacity fail to add housing units.

Our empirical analysis indicates that the small scale of many of the jurisdictions making land-use decisions is a significant factor—although certainly not the only one—influencing the Bay Area's undersupply of multifamily housing. In short, reducing the fragmentation of land-use decision-making may be necessary to ensure compact development, even if it is not—standing alone—sufficient.[1] Given the inability of a fragmented system of local government to confront region-wide problems, attention naturally turns to institutions that operate at the regional scale, and perhaps to state-level legislation as well. Chapter 3 provided a detailed analysis of six possible avenues for reform, ultimately recommending the regional housing appeals board as the most promising option in the short to medium term. In the long run, creation of an elective regional "umbrella" government, with significant implementation powers in the realm of land use and transportation, remains an attractive, if politically challenging, possibility.

Considering Potential Critiques and Objections

At least two elements of our argument are likely to draw significant objections from some quarters, both among academic scholars and among some citizen-activists. First, we concur with most mainstream analysts of urban housing policy that constrained supply is a fundamental part of the housing problem and that enabling substantially more construction—including market-rate projects built by private developers—is necessary to ameliorate the problem. But our assent to allowing market forces and profit-motivated builders to play a major role in satisfying residents' shelter needs will tend to arouse suspicion and dissent among those highly critical of the role that private capital has played in shaping U.S. metro areas. A venerable school of thought in urban political economy emphasizes the dark side of developer dominance and promarket policies in local politics.[2] From such a perspective, policies and institutions that enable local residents to defend the primacy of their "use value" of urban land would be preferable to allowing for-profit actors to construct projects that neighborhood residents do not want.

We also are not fans of giving business unfettered access to the levers of policy making. But we think the critique of supply-oriented approaches to the housing problem is misplaced, for a number of reasons. First, in economically vibrant regions, it is advantaged residents of affluent suburbs, not disadvantaged residents of inner-city neighborhoods, who have most heavily and successfully deployed "not in my backyard" or "use value" politics. Place-based activism by suburban homeowners tends to widen, rather than narrow, the already vast inequalities of the region. Such antidevelopment activism is bolstered by the institutional power of suburban municipalities—communities that for the most part have been shielded, because of their single-family zoning, from the potential entry of lower-income newcomers. As Manville and Monkkonen note, localism—the notion that incumbent residents should have a controlling voice in what gets built in a community—is hardly the same thing as equity: "Existing evidence suggests that exclusion and community self-determination are overwhelmingly tools for the privileged. Income segregation in the United States is driven less by society isolating the poor and more by the affluent isolating themselves. Whites are the most segregated racial group, and whiteness is itself a concept built on exclusion."[3]

Second, there is not necessarily an irresolvable conflict between a progressive, equity-oriented view of urban political economy and a favorable attitude toward making housing—especially multifamily housing—more abundant. If a goal of urban policy is to enable more upward mobility among low-income and minority residents, then enabling more multifamily housing to be constructed near plentiful job opportunities should be part of that strategy. Dense, infill housing near transit also is likely to generate less driving, and thus lower carbon emissions, than a similar number of housing units built in outlying, car-dependent locations (and indeed will generate less resource use per capita than existing single-family houses in the community).[4] Even if one would prefer that the public sector—or nonprofit groups or cooperatives—construct and operate that infill housing, an easing of single-family-only zoning and relaxation of cumbersome review processes for multifamily housing would still be needed to enable such housing.

Realistically, in the market-oriented economy that characterizes the United States now and in the foreseeable future, the overwhelming share of residential buildings very likely will continue to be built by private builders. This pattern has always been the case; nearly all the older housing units currently considered relatively affordable also were built for profit. But an *abundant housing* approach is quite consistent with efforts to increase the amount of social or public housing. Increasing housing supply also plays an important role in protecting vulnerable tenants from displacement. The current housing shortage in regions like the Bay Area is disruptive to the economic security of existing tenants because it makes them vulnerable to rapid increases in rents. Low-income renters increasingly find themselves competing with wealthier renters, as well-paid tech workers and young professionals seek housing in historically working-class neighborhoods due to the absence of rental options elsewhere. Indeed, a recent study finds that the Bay Area is one of the metropolitan regions where housing has tended to filter up, rather than filter down. That is, as housing units age in the Bay Area, they often transition from lower- to higher-income occupants.[5]

Building more housing—substantially more than in recent years—will be essential to dig out from the region's shortage. That said, in this study we have not attempted to fully diagnose the causes or consequences of the Bay Area's housing shortage or to estimate its absolute size, tasks which are beyond our scope and which various other studies have sought to accomplish.[6] Nor have we focused on the barriers specific to below-market-rate housing development, which faces all the challenges that beset producers of market-rate housing, plus many more.[7] We agree with many other observers that a comprehensive strategy likely is necessary to end the housing crisis in the Bay Area and other expensive regions. Elements of such a strategy could include substantially increased production at all price points, procedural and regulatory reforms, statewide fiscal reforms to incentivize localities to permit more housing, enhanced displacement protections and rent-increase limits for low-income tenants, increased public subsidies for housing, and a commitment to creating a stock of social housing.

A second likely line of attack regarding our recommended reforms comes from those who seek to uphold, and strengthen, local governments' autonomy. In recent years, there has been debate among scholars, as well as within politically progressive circles, about whether it is advisable to expand the role of state governments vis-à-vis their local governments. On one hand, some progressive voices seek state (or federal) intervention to restrain or strike down inequitable local policies, such as exclusionary zoning.[8] On the other hand, other progressives and legal scholars seek to bolster local power in the face of a growing number of state preemption laws in conservative states that have outlawed local regulatory activism on issues such as gun control or requiring businesses to provide paid leave.[9] With regard to the issue of housing, however, we think this conflict about local autonomy is resolvable. Scholars distinguish between *field preemption*, in which state governments "claim the field" and prevent local governments from legislating in certain policy areas, and the more defensible *floor preemption*, in which a state sets a minimum basic standard for local policy but allows for significant local flexibility in meeting the state standard.[10] California's recent state legislation aimed at boosting housing opportunity is mainly an example of floor preemption.

Similarly, our recommended institutional reform—a housing appeals process that sets out clear, bright-line standards for minimum levels of housing production—is a form of floor preemption rather than field preemption. Our Option Five would allow cities and counties to retain primary control over land-use planning as they decide *how* and *where* to best accommodate the necessary housing increase. Only if the localities fail to meet their production goals *and* deny proposed housing projects that would help them attain such goals would their denial of such projects be subject to being overturned by the regional appeals board. Meanwhile, the appeals board itself could function as an important venue for representing political interests whose voices are muted by the intensely local structure of suburban government, notably including the perspectives of renters, people lacking housing security, and those who would like to have the option to relocate to high-opportunity suburbs.

Majority public opinion in California appears to recognize some need to preempt local government in order to further housing production, according to evidence from a representative survey in 2019. Furthermore, statistical analysis of the poll data indicated that tenants, low-income people, and nonwhites tended to be most supportive of housing-related preemption, again suggesting that pressures to preserve local control of land use are *not* primarily a social equity–based movement.[11]

Strategic Considerations for Regional Reform

If regionalists or housing advocates take up the call for regional governance reform, it is advisable for them to be realistic about the many political obstacles to institutional change. The history of attempted metropolitan reorganizations, in the Bay Area and many other regions around the country, shows few examples of advocates making much headway at changing the localized system of land-use governance. For that reason, we conclude with four strategic considerations to bear in mind when attempting to enact and sustain a regional reform program.

Institutional Reform Is a Means to an End, Not an End in Itself

Reform advocates should identify a specific, salient policy problem that needs to be solved or an objective that needs to be attained, rather than just asserting the need for generic improvements in governance. Their campaign for change should be able to explain clearly how the new or altered governmental institution is likely to make progress on this front. Discussion of government structure can be vague, arcane, and downright boring for nonspecialists. By contrast, discussion of real-world regional problems and crises that resonate with citizens' lived experiences can draw more sympathetic attention. Reform advocates should stand ready to "attach" their well-formulated proposals to widely perceived problems, making the case that theirs is the logical solution.[12]

In the Bay Area, the main criterion for evaluating regional governmental structure should be its effects on shaping regional development, particularly on improving connections between housing and jobs for people at all income levels. Proposed reforms should be framed in reference to the housing crisis. Joël Thibert, reflecting on the quick success and legitimacy that BCDC gained in the 1960s in comparison to ABAG, writes, "It is easier for regional agencies to promote effective regional collaboration *when they are themselves perceived as effective*; this perception depends on whether they have a clear mandate and the ability to carry it out."[13] Unlike the vague responsibility of ABAG to promote regional cooperation and planning, for BCDC the

Bay itself was the "product" of its efforts. A cleaner Bay and the halt to Bay filling became visible to everyone, boosting BCDC's profile and reputation. As Assembly member John Knox described his 1970s-era approach to promoting regionalism, "The secret to it is identifying problems that have to be solved. And these are problems that are not strictly local situations but regional problems that go beyond the borders of a particular county or city. And once people realize that they all have to work together to get the best result . . . , that's what we're after." By contrast, reflecting on the overwhelming 1974 defeat of a proposed city-county consolidation by Sacramento-area voters, a conservative commentator argued, "The proponents of the measure were never able to articulate a good reason for a wholesale change in local government. There was no governmental crisis that precipitated the vote, no demonstrated inability of government to deal with problems and no consensus among the city's and county's elite on the need for major changes."[14]

In Designing New Regional Institutions, Allow for Some Open-Endedness in the Responsibilities Assigned

Prominent regional agencies in other regions did not acquire all their ultimate powers up front but were allowed to grow into their role. Thus, we suggest that the designers of any new Bay Area institution avoid being overly prescriptive in specifying the authority—or limits—of the regional agency. In the New York region, the Port Authority's enabling legislation was sufficiently flexible that once it had proved itself as a modernizer of ports and rail connections, it was granted additional, very significant regional powers—over tunnels, bridges, airports, and a rapid transit line. Portland's Metro, originating as a relatively empty-shell special district government, acquired new responsibilities—some minor, some region shaping—over its five decades of operation, particularly after its merger with CRAG. Demonstrating effectiveness early on can generate goodwill, and then, when political forces are in advantageous alignment, entrepreneurial leaders of regional organizations can position their agency as the logical unit to take on new responsibilities. In the Bay Area, the new BAHFA, with the cooperation of supportive state legislators, potentially could expand its future role in this manner.

To Influence a Metropolitan Region, Turn Attention toward the State Government

In the United States, local and regional governments are "creatures of the state," and state statutes created and altered some of the most important Bay Area institutions, including MTC and BCDC. In recent years, the most important policy changes enabling greater housing production have emerged from state legislation as well, as noted in our discussion of Option Four. Thus, although it is very important to build support for regional reform within the Bay Area, state government action ultimately is essential for all the options we have discussed, with the possible exception of city consolidations. Thus, advocates need to engage with state legislators from early on.

In a historical study, Zack Taylor finds that Canada succeeded to a substantially greater degree than the United States in creating and maintaining regional governing institutions to shape metropolitan growth, restraining outward sprawl and preserving the vitality of older centers.[15] He attributes much of this success to the hands-on role of Canada's provincial governments in the post–World War II period. In comparison to U.S. states, provinces (specifically Ontario and British Columbia) were both more *decisive* and more *resolute* in designing systems of regional governance. Notably, California currently has some of the characteristics that Taylor identifies as having been key for the Canadian provinces that successfully reorganized regional government in the postwar era: dominance by a single political party and a willingness among key state leaders to abridge home rule when appropriate. However, California lacks other features that helped the Canadian provinces take the lead in redesigning postwar regional governance, namely executive-centered policy making and high levels of public trust in government.

Recent changes in California's land-use laws and housing laws suggest both the potential for substantial reform and the limits on state-led reform. As discussed previously, California has strengthened the RHNA requirements and compelled local governments to become substantially more tolerant of ADUs. It has also empowered owner-occupiers of single-family homes to split their homes into duplexes and to split their lots (as long as it is at least 2,400 square feet) to build second units (which can be a duplex). According to some commentators, these changes amount to the end of single-family zoning in California.[16] On the other hand, efforts to set statewide floors on density restrictions in transit-accessible areas have repeatedly failed in the legislature. And state reforms concerning the RHNA requirements, ADUs, duplexes, and lot splits have triggered a campaign in support of a ballot measure that would amend the state constitution to effectively repeal these laws and drastically limit future state intervention in land-use regulation.[17]

Design Policies and Institutions to Create a Self-Reinforcing Politics

Reforms can be stymied if the coalition in favor of reform proves temporary and melts away after achieving the institutional changes it sought. By contrast, effective and durable laws often are those that create new, ongoing, support-ive political constituencies or empower existing ones. The new laws or insti-tutions created can do so by enhancing supporters' *incentives* to participate as well as their *ability* to participate. Political scientist Andrea Campbell pro-vides the classic example of the Social Security program. Social Security "helped transform senior citizens, who were once the least active age group in politics, into the most active by (a) giving them the resources of money and free time (the latter by making retirement a reality for most); (b) enhanc-ing their levels of political interest and efficacy by tying their well-being vis-ibly to a government program; and (c) creating incentives for interest groups to mobilize them by creating a political identity based on program recipi-ency."[18] In this way, well-designed laws and institutions can generate positive feedback, neutralizing the inevitable backlash against the reform and creat-ing a cascade or bandwagon effect that furthers the goals of proponents.[19]

Although California's recent state housing laws provide some new legal tools for housing advocates to challenge local governments (Option Four), they do not encourage the creation and maintenance of prohousing constitu-encies. Similarly, merging regional planning agencies (Option Two) is not likely to change the incentives for groups to form or participate in land-use disputes. In the near-term future, the state or regional appeals board (Op-tion Five) is the reform that seems most likely to create or energize a con-stituency that could help make the reform sustainable. Creating an appeals board would widen the scope of political conflict over housing beyond the neighborhood and municipal level, giving a seat at the table to interests that may be absent, ignored, or unpopular in local suburban land-use politics (e.g., affordable housing developers, nonprofit service providers, YIMBY groups, social equity organizations, and home builders). Although certain to arouse some significant opposition to its specific decisions within particular com-munities, the appeals board promises to create a new decision-making venue where these prohousing interests would be inclined to dig in and defend the process and the institution.

Similarly, a directly elected regional agency with land-use authority, al-though initially probably a much more difficult reform to enact, could create a self-reinforcing political dynamic over the long term. Candidates mount-ing campaigns for a *region-wide* office may find that supporting sustainable, compact development—including the construction of new housing in job-rich areas—comes to be viewed not only as good policy, but as good politics.

Technical Appendix

As noted in Chapter 2, jurisdictional size is one of many factors that may contribute to the siting of new housing generally—and new multifamily housing in particular. In order to estimate the role of jurisdictional population while controlling for other relevant socioeconomic, institutional, and geographic factors, we use regression analysis. Our sample consists of census tracts that are (a) located in California core-based statistical areas (CBSAs) with populations of at least five hundred thousand and (b) entirely contained within a single general-purpose local government (i.e., municipality or county).[1] Because we are focused on the prospects for multifamily infill development, we further restrict the sample to tracts defined by the U.S. Census Bureau as part of an "urbanized area."[2]

The Census Bureau's American Community Survey, which is the principal source of our data, is sample based. ACS estimates are therefore subject to sampling error. The ACS increases the reliability of tract-level estimates by pooling observations collected over a five-year period. Thus, the 2012 five-year ACS pools estimates from 2008 to 2012, and the 2018 five-year ACS pools estimates from 2014 to 2018. The dependent variable in our regression model is the change in multifamily units between the 2012 five-year ACS and the 2018 five-year ACS.[3] The control variables include a variety of attributes that are widely viewed as affecting housing development outcomes and are described in Table A.1.

Formally, our regression model is:

$$U_{tract,j,cbsa_t} - U_{tract,j,cbsa_{t-1}} = \rho W_{j,cbsa_{t-1}} + \beta X_{tract,j,cbsa_{t-1}} + \alpha_{cbsa} + \varepsilon_{tract,j,cbsa}$$

The subscripts index census tracts (*tract*), which are nested in jurisdictions (*j*), which are nested in CBSAs (*cbsa*). $U_{tract,j,cbsa}$ denotes the tract-level count of multifamily units, and the subscripts *t* and *t−1* denote, respectively, the 2014–2018 ACS and the 2008–2012

TABLE A.1 VARIABLES IN REGRESSION MODEL	
Variable	Definition
Tract level	
1. Change in multifamily units (dependent variable)	Change in multifamily units (2012 five-year ACS to 2018 five-year ACS)
2. Existing multifamily units	Count of multifamily units (2012 five-year ACS)
3. Median year built	Dichotomous variable indicating period during which the median-aged housing unit was constructed: (pre-1940, 1940–1959, 1960–1979, 1980–1999, or post-1999) (2012 five-year ACS)
4. Jobs within forty-five-minute drive	Jobs within forty-five-minute auto commute (one hundred thousands) (2010)
5. % vacant	Percentage of housing units that are vacant (2012 five-year ACS)
6. Average household size	Average number of persons per household (2012 five-year ACS)
7. Land area	Log of land area of tract (square miles) (2012)
8. % owner occupied	% of occupied housing units that are owner occupied (2012 five-year ACS)
9. % black/African American	% of population identifying as black or African American (2012 five-year ACS)
10. % Hispanic/Latino	% of population identifying as Hispanic or Latino (2012 five-year ACS)
11. % Asian	% of population identifying as Asian (2012 five-year ACS)
Jurisdiction level	
12. Population	Log of population (2012 five-year ACS)
13. County	= 1 if jurisdiction is a county
14. District elections	= 1 if a majority of the local legislature (city council or county board of supervisors) is elected by district

Sources: (1), (2), (3), (5), (6), (8), (9), (10), (11), (12): U.S. Census Bureau, American Community Survey; (7), (13): U.S. Census Bureau, 2012 TIGER/Line with Selected Demographic and Economic Data; (4): U.S. Environmental Protection Agency, Smart Location Database v. 2.0 (2013); (14): Nicholas Heidorn, California Common Cause, California Municipal Democracy Index (2016), available at https://perma.cc/4TXL-YATH.

ACS. $W_{j,cbsa_{t-1}}$ includes jurisdiction-level attributes that may affect the change in multifamily housing stock. $X_{t,j,cbsa_{t-1}}$ is a vector of relevant tract-level covariates. α_{cbsa} is a vector of CBSA fixed effects, and $\varepsilon_{track,j,cbsa}$ is the error term. The standard errors are clustered by *cbsa*.

We measure jurisdiction-level population in two different ways. In the first specification, we take the natural logarithm of population. In order to assess whether there are thresholds above or below which the relationship between population and housing development changes, the second specification includes a series of dichotomous variables, which equal one if a jurisdiction falls in the relevant population range and zero otherwise. Our results, reported in Table A.2, indicate that jurisdictions with populations of at least one hundred thousand are more accommodating of multifamily housing than jurisdictions with populations under fifty thousand and that jurisdictions in the population range of five hundred thousand to one million are the most accommodating of multifamily development.

TABLE A.2 REGRESSION RESULTS: TRACT-LEVEL CHANGE IN MULTIFAMILY UNITS

Tract-level covariates		
Existing multifamily units	0.033	0.028
	(0.044)	(0.042)
Median year built (dichotomous)		
Pre-1940	−201.896**	−226.502**
	(76.765)	(77.261)
1940–1959	−198.137**	−201.782**
	(88.053)	(89.688)
1960–1979	−185.762*	−187.511*
	(87.580)	(89.009)
1980–1999	−143.697*	−147.595*
	(75.407)	(76.476)
Jobs within forty-five-minute drive (one hundred thousands)	27.184***	27.662***
	(7.156)	(6.429)
% vacant	3.045***	2.948***
	(0.846)	(0.816)
Average household size	−3.994	−12.116
	(15.335)	(15.276)
Land area (log)	47.980***	50.161***
	(3.839)	(3.898)
% owner occupied	−0.347	−0.327
	(0.803)	(0.746)
% black/African American	0.217	0.311
	(0.126)	(0.248)
% Hispanic/Latino	0.354	0.538*
	(0.210)	(0.246)
% Asian	0.037	0.073
	(0.344)	(0.336)

(continued)

TABLE A.2 REGRESSION RESULTS: TRACT-LEVEL CHANGE IN MULTIFAMILY UNITS (*continued*)

Jurisdiction-level covariates		
Population (log)	14.038***	
	(2.934)	
Population range (dichotomous)		
Pop. ≥ 50,000 and < 100,000		17.165
		(14.294)
Pop. ≥ 100,000 and < 250,000		46.269**
		(17.529)
Pop. ≥ 250,000 and < 500,000		81.285***
		(19.650)
Pop. ≥ 500,000 and < 1,000,000		149.930***
		(19.836)
Pop. ≥ 1,000,000		88.084***
		(14.448)
County (dichotomous)	−47.844**	−37.146**
	(19.294)	(16.104)
District elections (dichotomous)	−14.759	−40.012***
	(8.277)	(7.774)
CBSA fixed effects	Yes	Yes
N	1,986	1,986
R²	0.12	0.13

* p < 0.1; ** p < 0.05; *** p < 0.01; standard errors clustered by CBSA in parentheses. Omitted median year built category is post-1999; omitted population category in the second specification is < 50,000. The dependent variable is the change in multifamily units between the 2012 five-year ACS and the 2018 five-year ACS.

Notes

INTRODUCTION

1. Data in this paragraph are from SPUR, "What It Will Really Take to Create an Affordable Bay Area," March 2020, available at https://perma.cc/MX7M-SXJ2.

2. For relevant data, see Metropolitan Transportation Commission and Association of Bay Area Governments, "Vital Signs: Housing Affordability," available at https://perma.cc/UB2D-5PUN, accessed June 17, 2021; San Francisco Foundation, "Bay Area Equity Atlas: Housing Burden," available at https://perma.cc/6Q89-2HLG, accessed June 17, 2021.

3. Population total calculated from 2021 data in State of California, Department of Finance, *Population Estimates for Cities, Counties, and the State: January 1, 2020 and 2021*, May 2021, available at https://www.dof.ca.gov/Forecasting/Demographics/Estimates/E-1/.

4. The other 9.3 percent of residents live in unincorporated areas, where county governments are the primary regulators of land use. Calculated from State of California, Department of Finance.

5. Following the longtime practice of scholars, policy makers, and journalists, we define the Bay Area as including the counties of Alameda, Contra Costa, Marin, Napa, San Francisco, San Mateo, Santa Clara, Solano, and Sonoma. As we describe in Chapter 2, however, in recent decades the region's housing shortfalls have pushed its commuter shed well beyond these traditional nine counties, as workers seek more affordable housing opportunities in outlying areas, particularly San Joaquin County.

6. Falk's story is recounted in Conor Dougherty, *Golden Gates: Fighting for Housing in America* (New York: Penguin Press, 2020), and in shorter form in Conor Dougherty, "Build Build Build," *New York Times*, February 13, 2020.

7. Steven Falk, Letter of Resignation, September 24, 2018, available at https://twitter.com/steven_b_falk/status/1045311105365504000. Two years earlier, City of Palo Alto planning and transportation commissioner Kate Vershov Downing resigned her post in

2016 citing similar reasons—and notably, her own family's inability to afford housing in that city. Kate Vershov Downing, "Letter of Resignation from the Palo Alto Planning and Transportation Commission," *Medium*, August 10, 2016, available at https://perma.cc /QMB7-EXXZ. Downing, however, was a volunteer commission member, while Falk was his city's chief administrative officer.

8. Assembly Bill 2923, 2017–2018 California General Assembly. As of 2020, BART was prioritizing development at several other stations rather than Lafayette, given the continued opposition of the city's elected officials. Lafayette is still, however, required to rezone the station area in accordance with the BART plan. Michaela Jarvis, "Home Is Where the BART Is: Transit Housing in the East Bay," *Diablo*, March 20, 2020; Pippa Fisher, "No Imminent Plans to Build on Lafayette BART-Owned Land," *Lamorinda Weekly*, March 6, 2019.

9. Bay Area Rapid Transit District, *TOD Guidelines and Procedures*, 2019, available at https://perma.cc/EU7D-9TLV; Benjamin Schneider, "BART Beats NIMBYs, But Not at Every Station," *SF Weekly*, July 22, 2020.

10. Vicki Been, Ingrid Gould Ellen, and Katherine O'Regan, "Supply Skepticism: Housing Supply and Affordability," *Housing Policy Debate* 29, no. 1 (2019): pp. 25–40; Evan Mast, "The Effect of New Market-Rate Housing Construction on the Low-Income Housing Market" (Working Paper No. 19-307, W. E. Upjohn Institute, 2019), available at https:// perma.cc/68YY-WJ3B.

CHAPTER 1

1. Data are from State of California, Department of Finance, *E-1 Population Estimates for Cities, Counties, and the State – January 1, 2019 and 2020*, May 2020, available at https:// perma.cc/4VJ6-Q33Q.

2. Paavo Monkkonen and Michael Manville, "Opposition to Development or Opposition to Developers? Experimental Evidence on Attitudes toward New Housing," *Journal of Urban Affairs* 41, no. 8 (2019): pp. 1123–1141, at p. 1125.

3. For the middle three quintiles of the household-wealth distribution, owner-occupied housing accounted for about 62 percent of household assets as of 2016. Edward N. Wolff, "Household Wealth Trends in the United States, 1962 to 2016: Has Middle Class Wealth Recovered?" (Working Paper No. 24085, National Bureau of Economic Research, 2017), table 6, available at https://perma.cc/BJ9L-KKVG.

4. William Fischel, *The Homevoter Hypothesis: How Home Values Influence Local Government Taxation, School Finance, and Land-Use Policies* (Cambridge, MA: Harvard University Press, 2001); William Fischel, "Political Structure and Exclusionary Zoning: Are Small Suburbs the Big Problem?," in *Fiscal Decentralization and Land Policies*, ed. Gregory K. Ingram and Yu-hung Hong (Cambridge, MA: Lincoln Institute of Land Policy, 2008), pp. 111–136.

5. Monkkonen and Manville, "Opposition to Development or Opposition to Developers?," p. 1126.

6. To be sure, renters may share these qualms about neighborhood disruption or anticipated disamenities. Michael Hankinson, "When Do Renters Behave Like Homeowners? High Rent, Price Anxiety, and NIMBYism," *American Political Science Review* 112, no. 3 (2018): pp. 473–493. But for homeowners, real or imagined disruptions that

might affect the value of their house can be the source of anxiety about the main or even the only significant investment in their portfolio.

7. Fischel, "Political Structure and Exclusionary Zoning."

8. John I. Carruthers, "Growth at the Fringe: The Influence of Political Fragmentation in United States Metropolitan Areas," *Papers in Regional Science* 82 (2003): pp. 475–499, at p. 477.

9. The importance of the "scope of conflict" in politics was highlighted in the classic book by E. E. Schattschneider, *The Semi-Sovereign People* (New York: Holt, Rinehart and Winston, 1960).

10. See, for example, J. Eric Oliver, "City Size and Civic Involvement in Metropolitan America," *American Political Science Review* 94, no. 2 (2000): pp. 361–373; Annie Gaardsted Frandsen, "Size and Electoral Participation in Local Elections," *Environment and Planning C: Government and Policy* 20 (2002): pp. 853–869; Zoltan L. Hajnal and Paul G. Lewis, "Municipal Institutions and Voter Turnout in Local Elections," *Urban Affairs Review* 38 (2003): pp. 645–668; João Cancela and Benny Geys, "Explaining Voter Turnout: A Meta-analysis of National and Subnational Elections," *Electoral Studies* 42 (2016): pp. 264–275.

11. Paul G. Lewis and Max Neiman, *Custodians of Place: Governing the Growth and Development of Cities* (Washington, DC: Georgetown University Press, 2009).

12. In reality, the council-manager plan of government, in which executive authority is vested in an appointed city manager, is overwhelmingly the norm in California municipalities, including those in the Bay Area. However, the authority and political strength of mayors tends to be more pronounced in the largest cities.

13. In some states, small suburban municipalities may derive a substantial share of their revenues from property taxes on industrial or office buildings, which in turn might insulate those cities somewhat from the antihousing entreaties of local homeowners. Even there, however, nonresidential property owners tend to be few in number as local *voters* (or may not reside locally at all), which should continue to give homeowners a potent advantage in local politics. In California cities, due to the strictures of the Proposition 13 property tax limitation passed in 1978, property taxes play a limited role in the finances of most local governments, giving local politicians even less reason to cater to the interests of industrialists who may favor a more abundant housing stock. More pertinent in California has been local government's favor toward retail development, given the existence of a local sales tax that is distributed to localities on a point-of-sale basis. Residential development, by comparison to retail, is often perceived as a fiscal money loser by local governments.

14. There is a potential flip side to this argument, however—namely, that local governments with greater capacity (i.e., more staff, higher revenues) might also have the capacity to devise additional regulatory hurdles for unwanted development, pursue litigation with developers, or evade state planning requirements. Although we cannot directly quantify these potential dampening effects of city size on residential development, our empirical analysis in Chapter 2 will indicate whether, on net, city size is positively or negatively related to growth in the number of multifamily housing units.

15. The limited available evidence suggests that, all else being equal, larger municipalities are better able to borrow money. Bill Simonsen, Mark Robbins, and Lee Helgerson, "The Influence of Jurisdiction Size and Sale Type on Municipal Bond Interest

Rates," *Public Administration Review* 61 (2001): pp. 709–717. It is also plausible that greater staff resources would enable larger municipalities to more effectively impose impact fees to support infrastructure necessitated by increases in population or density (e.g., new firefighting equipment needed for high-rise buildings).

16. California enacted legislation affirming cities' legal authority to adopt zoning in 1917. Elisa Barbour, *Metropolitan Growth Planning in California, 1990–2000* (San Francisco: Public Policy Institute of California, 2002), p. 12, available at https://perma.cc/TJW8-DE43.

17. See, e.g., Marc A. Weiss, "Urban Land Developers and the Origins of Zoning Laws: The Case of Berkeley," *Berkeley Planning Journal* 3, no. 1 (1986), pp. 7–25, esp. 18, available at https://escholarship.org/uc/item/26b8d8zh.

18. Jay Caspian Kang, "When a School Desegregates, Who Gets Left Behind?," *New York Times*, March 10, 2022; Nick Levinson and Marta Symkowick, "After Dearing: Residential Segregation and the Ongoing Effects on Piedmont," *Piedmont Exedra*, October 27, 2020, available at https://perma.cc/LAN4-GFW7; M. Bennett, "Racial Restrictions: Redlining in Piedmont, California before 1968," available at https://perma.cc/V29L-DXKR, accessed on April 3, 2022.

19. Tyler Reny and Benjamin Newman, "Protecting the Right to Discriminate: The Second Great Migration and Racial Threat in the American West," *American Political Science Review* 112 (2018): pp. 1104–1110.

20. Rolf Pendall, "Local Land Use Regulation and the Chain of Exclusion," *Journal of the American Planning Association* 66 (2000): pp. 125–142; Jonathan Rothwell and Douglas S. Massey, "The Effect of Density Zoning on Racial Segregation in U.S. Urban Areas," *Urban Affairs Review* 44, no. 6 (2009): pp. 779–806; Jessica Trounstine, *Segregation by Design: Local Politics and Inequality in American Cities* (New York: Cambridge University Press, 2018).

21. For the local angle, see Robert O. Self, *American Babylon: Race and the Struggle for Postwar Oakland* (Princeton, NJ: Princeton University Press, 2003). For national accounts of exclusionary zoning, see Michael N. Danielson, *The Politics of Exclusion* (New York: Columbia University Press, 1976); Trounstine, *Segregation by Design*.

22. Stephen Menendian et al., "Single-Family Zoning in the San Francisco Bay Area: Characteristics of Exclusionary Communities," Othering & Belonging Institute, University of California, Berkeley, October 7, 2020, available at https://perma.cc/486P-X68S.

23. Menendian et al., table 3.

24. Barbour, *Metropolitan Growth Planning*, p. 10.

25. See, generally, Alejandro E. Camacho and Nicholas J. Marantz, "Beyond Preemption, toward Metropolitan Governance," *Stanford Environmental Law Journal* 39 (2020): pp. 125–198, esp. 130–134.

26. Alex Schafran, *The Road to Resegregation: Northern California and the Failure of Politics* (Berkeley: University of California Press, 2018), p. 13.

27. Quoted in Stanley Scott and John C. Bollens, *Governing a Metropolitan Region: The San Francisco Bay Area* (Berkeley: University of California Institute of Governmental Studies, 1968), p. 7.

28. Although cities are numerous in California, it should be noted that many states, particularly in the Northeast and Midwest, are considerably more fragmented at the municipal level than California. While the state was adding many new cities in the early and mid-twentieth century, its population was growing at an even faster pace. Paul G.

Lewis, "The Durability of Local Government Structure: Evidence from California," *State and Local Government Review* 32, no. 1 (1999): pp. 34–48.

29. Carruthers, "Growth at the Fringe."

30. Calculated from the county-level listings of the Educational Data Partnership (a partnership of the California Department of Education, EdSource, and the Fiscal Crisis and Management Assistance Team/California School Information Services), available at https://perma.cc/85GX-QUT4, accessed February 22, 2021.

31. Notably, however, there is evidence that the centralization of school finance in California has attenuated these effects. Zachary Liscow, "The Efficiency of Equity in Local Government Finance," *New York University Law Review* 92, no. 6 (2017): pp. 1828–1908.

32. See, for example, Paul Warren and Julien LaFortune, *Achievement in California's Public Schools: What Do Test Scores Tell Us?* (San Francisco: Public Policy Institute of California, 2019), pp. 12–13, available at https://perma.cc/5RP9-33NX; Sean F. Reardon et al., *A Portrait of Educational Outcomes in California*, technical report, Stanford University and Policy Analysis for California Education, September 2018, p. 11, available at https://perma.cc/K6HQ-WSN6.

33. Calculated from the special-district database compiled by the California State Controller, updated as of January 10, 2019, available at https://perma.cc/FKT5-Y5RF. In our count of districts, we only include self-governing entities (labeled "independent districts" by the Controller) and not entities created by a city or county ("dependent" districts, which often share the same governing board as the city or county but have separate financial statements). Nor do we include joint powers authorities, which are entities jointly created by two or more cities or counties to carry out a particular responsibility.

34. For a classic statement of the public choice perspective, see Vincent Ostrom, Robert Bish, and Elinor Ostrom, *Local Government in the United States* (San Francisco: ICS Press, 1988).

35. Katherine Levine Einstein, David Glick, and Maxwell Palmer, *Neighborhood Defenders: Participatory Politics and America's Housing Crisis* (New York: Cambridge University Press, 2019).

36. See, e.g., the websites of the California Renters Legal Advocacy and Education Fund (CaRLA), available at https://perma.cc/35EQ-MKZ3, and YIMBY Law, available at https://perma.cc/DX5P-S7H9. For a discussion of the origins of CaRLA and other YIMBY groups, see Conor Dougherty, *Golden Gates: Fighting for Housing in America* (New York: Penguin Press, 2020).

37. This paragraph draws upon Paul G. Lewis, *Shaping Suburbia: How Political Institutions Organize Urban Development* (Pittsburgh, PA: University of Pittsburgh Press, 1996).

CHAPTER 2

1. Paul G. Lewis, "An Old Debate Confronts New Realities: Large Suburbs and Economic Development in the Metropolis," in *Metropolitan Governance: Conflict, Competition, and Cooperation*, ed. Richard C. Feiock (Washington, DC: Georgetown University Press, 2004), pp. 108–109.

2. As described in the technical appendix, we mitigate concerns arising from the sampling error inherent in the ACS estimates by analyzing only those tracts with high-reliability estimates.

3. Evan Mast, "Warding Off Development: Local Control, Housing Supply, and NIMBYs" (working paper, W. E. Upjohn Institute for Employment Research, July 2020), available at https://perma.cc/8Y7M-G8WM; Michael Hankinson and Asya Magazinnik, "The Supply–Equity Trade-Off: The Effect of Spatial Representation on the Local Housing Supply," conditionally accepted in the *Journal of Politics*, available at https://perma.cc/HNP8-628M, accessed on April 3, 2022.

4. The magnitude of the result may depend on the sample analyzed. As discussed in the appendix, our main sample consists of census tracts for which the ACS estimates are highly reliable.

5. Nicholas J. Marantz and Paul G. Lewis, "Jurisdictional Size and Residential Development: Are Large-Scale Local Governments More Receptive to Multifamily Housing?," *Urban Affairs Review* 58 (2022): pp. 732–766.

6. We aggregate block group-level data from the U.S. Environmental Protection Agency's Smart Location Database v. 2.0 (2013) to the city level, using the geographic correspondence engine provided by the Missouri Census Data Center. The Smart Location Database provides a measure of the number of jobs within a forty-five-minute commute of each census block group. We scale this measure by the proportion of a city's population residing in the block group and then aggregate the scaled values to the city level. We then divide this aggregated measure by city-level population and standardize so that the mean equals zero and the standard deviation equals one.

7. Robert C. Ellickson, "The Zoning Strait-Jacket: The Freezing of American Neighborhoods of Single-Family Houses" (Public Law Research Paper, Yale Law School, January 30, 2020), available at https://perma.cc/2WLP-BX6T.

8. Issi Romem, "America's New Metropolitan Landscape: Pockets of Dense Construction in a Dormant Suburban Interior," *Buildzoom*, February 1, 2018, available at https://perma.cc/AG6J-YSAV.

9. Metropolitan Transportation Commission, "Vital Signs: Housing Production," April 2020, available at https://perma.cc/YH7J-ZCGD.

10. Maggie Angst, "Apartment Boom in Central San Jose among the Top in U.S., Study Says," *Mercury News*, December 18, 2021.

11. The West Oakland case is described in Ayla Burnett and Semantha Norris, "Major West Oakland Housing Development Remains in Limbo," *The Oaklandside*, December 13, 2021, available at https://perma.cc/2UL7-4493. See also Natalie Orenstein, "'Depressingly' behind on Building Affordable Housing, Oakland Looks for More Money," *The Oaklandside*, June 23, 2021, available at https://perma.cc/XR3M-WRGT; Marisa Kendall, "Oakland Isn't Even Close to Meeting Its Lofty Low-Income Housing Goal," *Mercury News*, March 12, 2019.

12. On developer exactions and fees in California, see Sarah Mawhorter, David Garcia, and Hayley Raetz, *It All Adds Up: The Cost of Housing Development Fees in Seven California Cities* (Berkeley, CA: Terner Center for Housing Innovation, 2018), available at https://perma.cc/9A22-4MD2, and Marla Dresch and Steven Sheffrin, *Who Pays for Development Fees and Exactions?* (San Francisco: Public Policy Institute of California, 1997), available at https://perma.cc/FA9T-J6L2.

13. Fremont estimate is from Mawhorter et al., *It All Adds Up*; discussion of the incidence of the fees is in Dresch and Sheffrin, *Who Pays for Development Fees and Exactions?*

14. Elisabeth R. Gerber and Justin H. Phillips, "Direct Democracy and Land Use Policy: Exchanging Public Goods for Development Rights," *Urban Studies* 41, no. 2 (2004): pp. 463–479.

15. Alex Schafran, *The Road to Resegregation: Northern California and the Failure of Politics* (Berkeley: University of California Press, 2018), pp. 39–49.

16. William H. Lucy and David L. Phillips, *Confronting Suburban Decline: Strategic Planning for Metropolitan Renewal* (Washington, DC: Island Press, 2000).

17. Schafran, *Road to Resegregation*, p. 41, describes a "banana-shaped arc stretching from eastern Contra Costa County to southwestern Merced County" as the "Bay Area's primary growth frontier over the past two decades."

18. Paavo Monkkonen and Michael Manville, "Opposition to Development or Opposition to Developers? Experimental Evidence on Attitudes toward New Housing," *Journal of Urban Affairs* 41, no. 8 (2019): pp. 1123–1141.

19. On the shortcomings of single-function regional bodies, using greater Los Angeles as a case example, see Scott A. Bollens, "Fragments of Regionalism: The Limits of Southern California Governance," *Journal of Urban Affairs* 19, no. 1 (1997): pp. 105–122.

20. BART was initially planned as a wide-ranging system that would span the six inner counties of the region, but ultimately only the counties of Alameda, Contra Costa, and San Francisco "bought into" the system by approving a 1962 bond issue with an associated countywide tax. Thus, the system was scaled back to include only those three counties. As BART proved popular with riders, later agreements enabled its expansion into limited parts of San Mateo County and more recently Santa Clara County, but these counties lack voting representation on the BART board, given their initial rejection of the system. BART, "A History of BART: The Concept is Born," available at https://perma.cc/Q3JV-NLMK, accessed April 13, 2022.

21. San Francisco Bay Conservation and Development Commission, *History of the San Francisco Bay Conservation and Development Commission*, available at https://perma.cc/7YL3-UMWK, accessed February 22, 2021.

22. Scholarly opinions and participants' recollections differ as to whether ABAG originated as a reluctant response to an outside threat—a bill in the legislature to create a multipurpose regional transportation agency, to be called the Golden Gate Authority—or whether ABAG arose due to genuine enthusiasm among local officials for regional coordination and discussion. Compare Louise Nelson Dyble, "The Defeat of the Golden Gate Authority: A Special District, a Council of Governments, and the Fate of Regional Planning in the San Francisco Bay Area," *Journal of Urban History* 34, no. 2 (2008): pp. 287–308 (arguing that ABAG's formation was an attempt to thwart the state's creation of a regional authority) with Joël Thibert, *Governing Urban Regions through Collaboration: A View from North America* (New York: Routledge, 2016), pp. 101–142 (noting preexisting interlocal cooperation among mayors and describing some veins of support for stronger regionalism among ABAG's early board members).

23. Elisa Barbour, *Metropolitan Growth Planning in California, 1990–2000* (San Francisco: Public Policy Institute of California, 2002), pp. 28–29, available at https://perma.cc/TJW8-DE43.

24. Revan Tranter, *ABAG: A Concise History Celebrating 40 Years of Service* (Berkeley: University of California Institute of Governmental Studies, 2001), pp. 2–3, available at https://perma.cc/3NQ3-THR5; Thibert, *Governing Urban Regions*.

25. Similarly, state law has defined "regions" as counties in another important realm: the review of proposals for local boundary changes (i.e., annexations) and formation of new governments, such as municipal incorporations or creation of new special districts. The state created a new set of entities in 1963 to review and decide upon such boundary and service-area issues, called Local Agency Formation Commissions (LAFCOs). However, California vested LAFCO power at the scale of the county, not the metropolitan region, so there are nine separate LAFCOs operating in the Bay Area. State law governing LAFCOs was substantially revised in 2000, but the county-level scale of LAFCOs was left in place. See State of California, Commission on Local Governance in the 21st Century, *Growth within Bounds: Planning California Governance for the 21st Century*, January 2000, pp. 25–28, available at https://perma.cc/8X45-CRSA; Barbour, *Metropolitan Growth Planning*, pp. 26–28, 62; California Senate Governance and Finance Committee, *50 Years of LAFCOs*, December 2013, available at https://perma.cc/X42Z-SZ74.

26. The two quotes are, respectively, from Amber E. Crabbe et al., "Local Transportation Sales Taxes: California's Experiment in Transportation Finance," *Public Budgeting & Finance*, Fall 2005, pp. 91–121, at p. 111; and Judith E. Innes and Judith Gruber, "Planning Styles in Conflict: The Metropolitan Transportation Commission," *Journal of the American Planning Association* 71, no. 2 (2005): pp. 177–188, at p. 179.

27. ABAG also suffered from the ending of the federal government's Section 701 planning grants program, the expiration of a federal environmental management grant, and the passage of the statewide property tax limitation Proposition 13, all in rapid succession in the late 1970s. Proposition 13 created financial strains for ABAG's local government members, which then voted to sharply cut their membership dues in the association. As a result of these fiscal tides, ABAG was forced to reduce its staff size by about three-quarters by the early 1980s. MTC, *Bay Area Regionalism Oral History: Revan Tranter*, video, 2011, available at https://perma.cc/6DP5-VBTE (hereafter cited as Tranter Oral History).

28. Tranter Oral History; Tranter, *ABAG: A Concise History*, p. 8.

29. Harriet Nathan and Stanley Scott, eds., *Toward a Bay Area Regional Organization: Report of the Conference* (Berkeley: University of California Institute of Governmental Studies, 1969).

30. In 1969, ABAG tried again with a proposal for "regional home rule" and integration with the BAAQMD. See Stanley Scott and John C. Bollens, *Governing a Metropolitan Region: The San Francisco Bay Area* (Berkeley: University of California Institute of Governmental Studies, 1968), pp. 4, 92–96; Thibert, *Governing Urban Regions*.

31. Barbour, *Metropolitan Growth Planning*, p. 36.

32. MTC, *Bay Area Regionalism Oral History: John Knox*, video, 2011, available at https://perma.cc/Z5C5-TUPK.

33. MTC, *Tranter Oral History*.

34. Thibert, *Governing Urban Regions*; Joseph E. Bodovitz, "Bay Area Regionalism: Can We Get There?," *The Urbanist*, September 2003, available at https://perma.cc/U9PM-VB2S.

35. MTC, *Bay Area Regionalism Oral History: Rod Diridon, Sr.*, video, 2011, available at https://perma.cc/BKC7-EDBS. Diridon had served at various times as ABAG president, MTC chair, and a Santa Clara County supervisor.

36. The bills would have renamed the new entity, alternately, the Bay Area Land Use and Transportation Commission or the Regional Growth Council. According to the bill

analysis from the legislative committee staff, "Not a single city or county in the Bay Area supports SB 864, and the great majority of them are formally opposed to it. SB 864 is also opposed by the region's mayors' conferences and a number of transit districts." California Assembly Committee on Local Government, "Bill Analysis, S.B. 864," August 19, 2002, available at https://perma.cc/EMD6-44UT.

37. SB 828, 2003–2004 Leg. (Cal. 2004), also authored by Sen. Torlakson.

38. MTC, "ABAG and MTC Staff Join Forces," October 13, 2017, available at https://perma.cc/QJK5-EH3Z.

39. ABAG, "PDA - Priority Development Areas," available at https://perma.cc/TW6U-PNBJ., accessed February 23, 2021.

40. MTC, "Priority Development Areas: Top 5 Frequently Asked Questions," available at https://perma.cc/3EWW-VG78, accessed February 23, 2021.

41. MTC, "Priority Development Areas."

42. Julie Pierce, "The Future of SB 375 Implementation and Regional Planning," *Western City*, March 1, 2015, available at https://perma.cc/2WSE-F53S.

43. MTC and ABAG, *Plan Bay Area 2040, Final Plan: Action Plan*, 2019, available at https://perma.cc/3BKV-35KH; Thibert, *Governing Urban Regions*.

44. MTC, *Bay Area Regionalism Oral History: Henry Gardner*, video, 2011, available at https://perma.cc/CYG9-X6GL.

45. MTC and ABAG, *Plan Bay Area 2040, Implementation Plan*, 2021, available at https://perma.cc/8EE3-5KGB.

46. The Committee to House the Bay Area, *CASA Compact: A 15-Year Emergency Policy Package to Confront the Housing Crisis in the San Francisco Bay Area*, 2019, available at https://perma.cc/JUD9-4WXJ.

47. Assembly Bill 1487, 2019–2020 General Assembly.

48. Bodovitz, "Bay Area Regionalism: Can We Get There?"

49. Barbour, *Metropolitan Growth Planning*, p. viii.

50. At this writing, five of the twenty-one members of the MTC governing board also sit on the ABAG Executive Board.

51. Revan Tranter, "Maintain the Local Voice in Bay Area Land Use—Oppose MTC Plan," *San Francisco Chronicle*, May 18, 2016.

52. Paul G. Lewis and Elisa Barbour, *California Cities and the Local Sales Tax* (San Francisco: Public Policy Institute of California, 1999), available at https://perma.cc/UU75-3HAC; Jeffrey I. Chapman, *Proposition 13: Some Unintended Consequences* (San Francisco: Public Policy Institute of California, 1998), available at https://perma.cc/YTM5-GAK5.

53. SB 167, 2017–2018 Leg.

54. See Christopher S. Elmendorf et al., "Making It Work: Legal Foundations for Administrative Reform of California's Housing Framework," *Ecology Law Quarterly* 47 (2020): pp. 973–1060.

CHAPTER 3

1. For a taxonomy assessing the relevant trade-offs, see Alejandro E. Camacho and Robert L. Glicksman, *Reorganizing Government: A Functional and Dimensional Framework* (New York: NYU Press, 2019).

2. Nicholas J. Marantz and Paul G. Lewis, "Jurisdictional Size and Residential Development: Are Large-Scale Local Governments More Receptive to Multifamily Housing?," *Urban Affairs Review* 58 (2022): pp. 732–766.

3. California's local government law directs LAFCOs in each county, when considering a "consolidation of two or more cities or districts, to determine which city or district shall be the consolidated, successor city or district." California Assembly Committee on Local Government, *Guide to the Cortese-Knox-Hertzberg Local Government Reorganization Act of 2000* (Sacramento, CA, 2019), p. 49, section 56375, available at https://perma .cc/2JH8-LY3J. This language appears to presume that an existing city will always be the "successor," rather than—as in some states—allowing for the creation of a wholly new city and disincorporating each of the existing cities involved in the consolidation. The act does, however, allow for the consolidated city to choose a new name (p. 86). The successor city's ordinances remain in effect, while the "predecessor" city's ordinances are "repealed – except for assessments, zoning, etc." Whether the new city is deemed a general-law city or a charter city (the latter status provides more local discretion for policy making and governmental structure) depends on which category the successor city had prior to the merger. See Michael G. Colantuono, "Consolidation and Disincorporation of Cities" (presentation to the California Association of Local Agency Formation Commissions, June 29, 2012), available at https://perma.cc/XRZ6-FHFZ.

4. See Table A.2 in the appendix for the statistical results, in which district elections are negatively correlated with multifamily housing production at the census-tract level, although this relationship only is statistically significant in one of our two specifications. See also Michael Hankinson and Asya Magazinnik, "The Supply–Equity Trade-Off: The Effect of Spatial Representation on the Local Housing Supply," conditionally accepted in the *Journal of Politics*, available at https://perma.cc/HNP8-628M, accessed April 3, 2022. Thanks to Albert Solé-Ollé for suggesting this point about consolidation.

5. While some of these one-hundred-thousand-plus cities are in job-rich parts of the region (e.g., Sunnyvale, San Mateo, Berkeley), others are satellite cities located far from the Bay Area's main employment concentrations (e.g., Santa Rosa, Antioch, Vacaville).

6. The city of San Francisco, and what was then the northern portion of San Francisco County, merged in 1856, at which time the state legislature detached the other, southern portion of San Francisco County and renamed it San Mateo County. That event now seems largely lost in the mists of time. If, a few decades later, San Mateo County communities along the northern half of the current-day Caltrain line had merged into one large city, in all likelihood these areas would still have developed the economic centrality and modern public services they enjoy today (and perhaps more, given the presence of a municipal government with greater capacity). The resulting arrangement would today seem just as natural as San Francisco's. Residents might identify their loyalties with "Peninsula City" or some other such large-scale municipality, rather than with the much smaller-scale communities they currently reside in, but life (and local democracy) would have gone on. Land-use patterns, however, might well have evolved in a different fashion, with more consideration given to balancing burgeoning job growth with housing development.

7. Although about ten small cities consolidated with the City of Los Angeles in its early years (including the well-known, previously separate communities of Hollywood and Venice), the city gained most of its prodigious area through annexation of unincorporated

land. Richard Bigger and James Kitchen, *Metropolitan Los Angeles: How the Cities Grew* (Los Angeles, CA: Haynes Foundation, 1952, p. 36). Municipal consolidations have been virtually nonexistent in California in recent decades, with the last apparently being San Jose's absorption of the tiny city of Alviso in 1968. Peter M. Detwiler, "Disincorporations in California," June 29, 2012, available at https://perma.cc/8Z3H-3SES. As described in the following, a handful of U.S. central cities have merged with their *counties* (rather than with neighboring cities) in the postwar period.

8. A notable exception is the unincorporated community of Castro Valley (approximate population sixty-three thousand), which is located in the East Bay alongside the cities of San Leandro and Hayward and has voted down proposals to incorporate as a city. Much further from the center of the region are unincorporated areas functioning as bedroom communities and lacking close access to job centers (e.g., Discovery Bay in eastern Contra Costa County).

9. Assembly Committee on Local Government, *Guide to the Cortese-Knox-Hertzberg Act*, p. 89, section 56734.

10. For examples of the complexities of combining municipalities in other states, see, regarding Pennsylvania, Kate Liao Shaffner, "Municipal Mergers and Consolidations: Solution for Distressed Municipalities?," *WHYY*, September 5, 2014, available at https://perma.cc/P34K-WA8W, and regarding New Jersey, John Van Vliet, "The Covid-19 Era Case for Municipal Consolidation," *Insider NJ*, May 14, 2020, available at https://perma.cc/UT5E-8LKJ. Recent consolidations have been exceedingly rare in both states, even though the case for such mergers seems even stronger there than in California.

11. Vincent Ostrom, Robert Bish, and Elinor Ostrom, *Local Government in the United States* (San Francisco, CA: ICS Press, 1988); Poul Erik Mouritzen, "City Size and Citizens' Satisfaction: Two Competing Theories Revisited," *European Journal of Political Research* 17, no. 6 (1989): pp. 661–688; Paul Teske et al., "Establishing the Micro Foundations of a Macro Theory: Information, Movers, and the Competitive Local Market for Public Goods," *American Political Science Review* 87 (1993): pp. 702–713. But see also William Lyons, David Lowery, and Ruth DeHoog, *The Politics of Dissatisfaction: Citizens, Services, and Urban Institutions* (Armonk, NY: M. E. Sharpe, 1992).

12. Suzanne M. Leland and Kurt Thurmaier, eds., *City–County Consolidation: Promises Made, Promises Kept?* (Washington, DC: Georgetown University Press, 2010); Dagney Faulk and Georg Grassmueck, "City-County Consolidation and Local Government Expenditures," *State and Local Government Review* 44, no. 3 (2012): pp. 196–205.

13. Assembly Committee on Local Government, *Guide to the Cortese-Knox-Hertzberg Act*, see esp. p. 97, section 56766, and pp. 174–175, section 57177.5.

14. Bonnie S. Wang et al., "Drive Until You Qualify: Exploring Long Commutes in a High Housing Cost Region," SSRN, April 4, 2022, available at http://dx.doi.org/10.2139/ssrn.4074809.

15. State of California, Department of Housing and Community Development, *ABAG Final Regional Housing Need Determination*, June 9, 2020, available at https://perma.cc/RBM6-P54W.

16. Imagine if MTC not only decided on the priority for BART extensions versus bike trails or highway interchanges but also "owned" the BART system, having to seek revenues from fares and engaging directly in labor negotiations with BART's unionized employees.

17. Donald Chisholm, *Coordination without Hierarchy: Informal Structures in Multi-organizational Systems* (Berkeley: University of California Press, 1989).

18. Granted, each locality is required by state law to show how the housing element of its general plan has the potential to accommodate the targeted numbers of housing units assigned to it by ABAG under RHNA. But compliance or noncompliance with RHNA requirements is evaluated by the California Department of Housing and Community Development, not ABAG. During some time periods, many localities have been noncompliant with the housing element requirement, with minimal repercussions. See the section on Option Four in this chapter for further discussion of RHNA.

19. Rebecca Lewis, Gerrit-Jan Knaap, and Jungyul Sohn, "Managing Growth with Priority Funding Areas: A Good Idea Whose Time Has Yet to Come," *Journal of the American Planning Association* 75, no. 4 (2009): pp. 457–478.

20. Martin A. Bierbaum, "State Plan and Smart Growth Implementation: The New Jersey Case," in Gerrit Knaap et al., eds., *Incentives, Regulations and Plans: The Role of States and Nation-States in Smart Growth Planning* (Cheltenham, UK: Edward Elgar, 2007), chap. 12; Jason Sartori, Terry Moore, and Gerrit Knaap, "Indicators of Smart Growth in Maryland" (University of Maryland, National Center for Smart Growth Research and Education, January 2011), p. 48, available at https://perma.cc/A3LR-ZU2W.

21. The mayors of the three primary central cities—Oakland, San Jose, and San Francisco—are each granted an appointee on the commission, with the mayors of the first two cities naming themselves to the position. In other cases, municipal officials are selected for a commission seat by a vote of their counterparts within their county. See MTC, "Commissioners," available at https://perma.cc/Y3UC-JYXM (click on the tab "How Commissioners Are Selected"), accessed February 23, 2021.

22. In addition to its thirty-four-member Executive Board, ABAG has a General Assembly that represents each and every member government. The General Assembly meets annually to review bylaws, the association's budget, and a work plan. See ABAG, "How We Govern," available at https://perma.cc/SF67-8REL, accessed February 23, 2021.

23. Residents, of course, are free to attend public meetings of the regional governing boards, an opportunity that actually became somewhat easier for some residents in far-flung communities during the COVID-19 pandemic, since they could participate remotely.

24. Quoted in Rachel Swan, "North Bay Councilman Spurned, Again, for Housing Decision," *San Francisco Chronicle*, February 1, 2019.

25. There is another problem of constituent-unit representation that is distinct from the problem of lack of direct representation of regional citizens: The boards may give excessive voting power to representatives of small municipalities or small counties, thereby underweighting the votes of representatives of large cities or large counties. See Paul G. Lewis, "Regionalism and Representation: Measuring and Assessing Representation in Metropolitan Planning Organizations," *Urban Affairs Review* 33, no. 6 (1998): pp. 839–853, and the proposal for "qualified majority voting" in Gerald E. Frug, "Beyond Regional Government," *Harvard Law Review* 115, no. 7 (2002): pp. 1763–1836, at pp. 1797–1805.

26. See Harriet Nathan and Stanley Scott, eds., *Toward a Bay Area Regional Organization: Report of the Conference* (Berkeley: University of California Institute of Governmental Studies, 1969).

27. The U.S. Supreme Court had only a few years earlier ruled that state and local legislative bodies must provide for "one person, one vote" representation. Reynolds v. Sims, 377 U.S. 533 (1964).

28. G. Ross Stephens and Nelson Wikstrom, *Metropolitan Government and Governance: Theoretical Perspectives, Empirical Analysis, and the Future* (New York: Oxford University Press, 1999).

29. Then Assembly member (and future San Francisco mayor) Willie Brown told the Berkeley regional governance conference in 1968 that "there must be an amalgam of metropolitan centralism with city or community decentralism, in order to protect the rights of minority communities to a degree of self-management, as well as a degree of representation in the larger regional issues." But he warned that minority power would be compromised by the "superficially attractive amalgamation of existing communities in the region into one big super government or 'Metro.'" Willie Brown, "Regional Government: Impact on the Poor," in Nathan and Scott, *Toward a Bay Area Regional Organization*, p. 94.

30. Frug, "Beyond Regional Government," noted that "the two-tier solution is embraced by virtually every major contemporary proponent of regional government" (p. 1776) and recommended a modified form of bi-level regional government inspired by the representation of nations in the European Union.

31. The potential functions ranged from air-pollution control and water supply to civil defense and "any other areawide function requested by the residents and leadership" of the region. See Stanley Scott and John C. Bollens, "Problems of Organizing a Regional Government," in Nathan and Scott, *Toward a Bay Area Regional Organization*, p. 225.

32. Jameson W. Doig, *Empire on the Hudson: Entrepreneurial Vision and Political Power at the Port of New York Authority* (New York: Columbia University Press, 2001).

33. Amy Howe, "Argument Preview: 'Bridgegate' Scandal Comes to the Court," *SCOTUSblog*, January 7, 2020, available at https://perma.cc/B4HH-BWB7.

34. Metro's territory includes portions of the counties of Multnomah, Clackamas, and Washington that constitute the main urbanized and urbanizing area on the Oregon side of the Columbia River. See Metro, "What Is Metro?," available at https://perma.cc/8NJ6-B29B, accessed March 14, 2021. However, the Vancouver, Washington, portion of the region is not governed by Metro, and in recent years the federal government also has added two outlying counties in Oregon to the federally defined metropolitan area. The following discussion of Metro's history and activities draws upon Paul G. Lewis, *Shaping Suburbia: How Political Institutions Organize Urban Development* (Pittsburgh, PA: University of Pittsburgh Press, 1996), chap. 4 and 6; Carl Abbott, "Metro Regional Government," *The Oregon Encyclopedia*, Oregon Historical Society, 2018, available at https://perma.cc/ET7D-YRJ2; and Zack Taylor, *Shaping the Metropolis: Institutions and Urbanization in the United States and Canada* (Montreal, Canada: McGill-Queen's University Press, 2019), chap. 7.

35. Although empowered to take over the operations of the region's mass transit system, Metro has left operational responsibility in the hands of a separate special district, Tri-Met, while Metro coordinates and prioritizes transportation funding as the region's metropolitan planning organization.

36. Examining Metro's annual budget in relation to that of the Bay Area's corresponding regional agencies is a bit of an apples-to-oranges comparison, due to their differing

responsibilities. But given the much larger population of the Bay Area, such a comparison indicates the proportionally greater prominence of Metro. ABAG's 2019–2020 budgeted expenditures were $3.7 million for its main planning program, plus $26.8 million for its BayREN regional energy-efficiency partnership and $20.1 million for its Bay Area Estuary Partnership. ABAG, *ABAG Budget and Work Program, Approved, FY 2019–20*, available at https://perma.cc/FGK6-727L, accessed March 14, 2021. MTC's 2019–2020 operating budget was $67.8 million, plus $33.7 million for its Bay Area Forward program. MTC, *Budget FY 2019–20, Attachment A*, June 5, 2019, available at https://perma.cc/8B6C-85B3.

37. Most of Metro's property taxes are devoted to specific voter-approved expenditure programs such as those for open space or affordable housing, but a lesser amount derives from a permanent levy designated for general operations. Budgetary figures are from Metro, *Adopted Budget, FY 2019–20*, June 20, 2019, available at https://perma.cc/T2SJ-F5Y3.

38. Taylor has described how Metro's democratically elected nature ("input legitimacy"), the openness and transparency of its procedures ("throughput legitimacy"), and its organizational performance in achieving goals valued in the region ("output legitimacy") have helped it attain considerably more public acceptance than the other main exemplar of regional-level decision-making in the United States, the Twin Cities Metropolitan Council. Zack Taylor, "Pathways to Legitimacy," *Planning Theory* 18, no. 2 (2019): pp. 214–236.

39. Nathan and Scott, *Toward a Bay Area Regional Organization*.

40. Institute for Local Government, "The Basics of SB 375," 2015, available at https://perma.cc/RG24-PDE5; Elisa Barbour, "Evaluating Sustainability Planning under California's Senate Bill 375," *Transportation Research Record*, no. 2568 (2016): pp. 17–25.

41. Scott Bollens, "State Growth Management: Intergovernmental Frameworks and Policy Objectives," *Journal of the American Planning Association* 58 (1992): pp. 454–466.

42. Metro's jurisdiction includes 1.5 million residents living in three counties and twenty-four incorporated cities. There are eight other cities located (at least partially) within the three counties but outside Metro's boundaries. Metro, "What Is Metro?"

43. Cal. Gov't Code § 65584.01(b), as amended by SB 828, 2017–2018 Leg. (Cal. 2018).

44. Cal. Gov't Code § 65584.04(e).

45. Christopher S. Elmendorf, "Beyond the Double Veto: Housing Plans as Preemptive Intergovernmental Compacts," *Hastings Law Journal* 77, no. 1 (2019): pp. 79–150, esp. pp. 116–122.

46. State of California, Department of Housing and Community Development, *ABAG Final Regional Housing Need Determination*.

47. State of California, Department of Housing and Community Development, "Re: Regional Housing Need Determination for Housing Element Updates," February 24, 2012, available at https://perma.cc/XHB3-Q5HE.

48. Christopher S. Elmendorf et al., *Regional Housing Need in California: The San Francisco Bay Area*, (Los Angeles, CA: UCLA Lewis Center for Regional Policy Studies, 2020), available at https://escholarship.org/uc/item/69j2b63r; Sara Ogilvie, "Planning to Fail," *Medium*, June 24, 2020, available at https://perma.cc/DDY7-AWED.

49. UCLA cityLAB, *Building an ADU: Guidebook to Accessory Dwelling Units in the City of Los Angeles*, 2017, p. 3, available at https://perma.cc/WL2Z-6URP.

50. See, e.g., Kenneth Stahl (@kookie13), Twitter, June 28, 2020, 3:54 p.m., available at https://twitter.com/kookie13/status/1277374937515192320.

51. Nicholas J Marantz and Huixin Zheng, "State Affordable Housing Appeals Systems and Access to Opportunity: Evidence from the Northeastern United States," *Housing Policy Debate* 30, no. 3 (2020): pp. 370–395; see also Carolina K. Reid, Carol Galante, and Ashley F. Weinstein-Carnes, "Addressing California's Housing Shortage: Lessons from Massachusetts Chapter 40B," *Journal of Affordable Housing & Community Development Law* 25 (2017): pp. 241–274.

52. Units satisfying the fair-share criteria include those with prices or rents restricted by deed to households with incomes at or below 80 percent of the area median, as well as market-rate units in rental projects where 20–25 percent of the units are deed-restricted below-market-rate units. The safe harbor applies to municipalities that have received state approval for a housing production plan and increase their below-market-rate housing stock by a statutorily specified annual percentage.

53. See, e.g., SB 35 (Wiener), 2017–2018 Leg., Reg. Sess. (Cal. 2017).

54. California's Housing Accountability Act does provide a zoning override for projects in which 20 percent of the units are below-market-rate units, if a jurisdiction "has failed to identify in . . . its housing element sites that . . . are sufficient to provide for the jurisdiction's" allocated share of housing units. California Government Code § 65589.5(d)(5)(B). But cities have a variety of legal arguments at their disposal to counter claims relying on this provision of the Housing Accountability Act, which may account for developers' neglect of this potential zoning override. Christopher S. Elmendorf, "A Primer on California's 'Builder's Remedy' for Housing-Element Noncompliance" (University of California, Davis, School of Law, March 29, 2022), available at https://perma .cc/8A67-BZS2.

55. For example, SB 35 removes the requirement for analysis under the California Environmental Quality Act for certain housing projects that would help a locality fulfill its allocated share of regional housing needs, thereby expediting the review process.

56. Zoning Board of Appeals of Canton vs. Housing Appeals Committee, 76 Mass. App. Ct. 467 (2010).

57. Aaron Gornstein and Ann Verrilli, *Mixed-Income Housing in the Suburbs: Lessons from Massachusetts* (Boston, MA: Citizens' Housing and Planning Association, 2006), p. 42, available at https://perma.cc/7PGX-JFVL.

58. Secretary of the Commonwealth of Massachusetts, "2010 Statewide Question #2," available at https://perma.cc/26CE-PBCT.

59. Reid et al., "Addressing California's Housing Shortage."

60. See Opticos Design, "Missing Middle Housing," 2021, https://perma.cc/7NPR -626Y.

61. For example, each multifamily or townhome market-rate unit could count for one unit, each moderate-income unit (affordable at 30 percent of household income to households earning 80–120 percent of area median income, or AMI) could count for one and a half units, each low-income unit (affordable at 50–80 percent of AMI) could count for two units, each very low-income unit (affordable at 30–50 percent of AMI) could count for three units, and each extremely low-income unit (affordable at 0–30 percent of AMI) could count for four units.

62. Reid et al., "Addressing California's Housing Shortage."

63. SB 744 (Dunn), 2003–2004 Leg., Reg. Sess. (Cal. 2003); AB 1585 (Bloom), 2017–2018 Leg., Reg. Sess. (Cal. 2017).

64. SB 827 (Wiener), 2017–2018 Leg., Reg. Sess. (Cal. 2018); SB 50 (Wiener), 2019–2020 Leg., Reg. Sess. (Cal. 2020).

65. Michael N. Danielson, *The Politics of Exclusion* (New York: Columbia University Press, 1976).

66. California Legislative Analyst's Office, "Common Claims about Proposition 13," 2016, p. 27, available at https://perma.cc/WEU3-9L8S.

67. California Legislative Analyst's Office, pp. 33–36.

68. California Legislative Analyst's Office, pp. 11–12.

69. Marla Dresch and Steven Sheffrin, *Who Pays for Development Fees and Exactions?* (San Francisco: Public Policy Institute of California, 1997), p. 8, available at https://perma.cc/FA9T-J6L2.

70. Dresch and Sheffrin, p. 11.

71. Dresch and Sheffrin, pp. 75–76.

72. Christopher S. Elmendorf and Darien Shanske, "Auctioning the Upzone," *Case Western Reserve Law Review* 70, no. 3 (2020): pp. 513–572 (see, especially, pp. 521–524).

73. Elmendorf and Shanske, pp. 524–527.

74. Elmendorf and Shanske, pp. 530–531.

75. Public Policy Institute of California, *Proposition 13: 40 Years Later*, June 2018, available at https://perma.cc/33Q9-KAY6. Relatively narrow reforms are more plausible. Such reforms include removing protections for commercial property and limiting the ability of homeowners to pass on their assessments to their children. (These two reforms were addressed, respectively, by Propositions 15 and 19 on the November 2020 statewide ballot. Proposition 15 was defeated and Proposition 19 passed, both by fairly narrow margins.)

76. As of 2015, 18 percent of local property tax revenues statewide went to cities, with larger shares going to school districts and county governments. See California Legislative Analyst's Office, "Local Governments' Services and Their Property Tax Revenue," 2015, available at https://perma.cc/4YKQ-RZQK. The exact proportions can differ quite considerably from city to city, reflecting historical differences in reliance on property taxes at the time of Proposition 13's passage.

77. For example, California's 2017 passage of an increase in the gasoline tax, much of which is shared with cities on the basis of their population size, approximately doubled the flow to cities of state shared revenues of this type. However, these revenues are earmarked for local streets and roads, rather than representing an increase in local discretionary revenue, suggesting that the impact of this fiscal change on city governments' receptivity to new housing is probably limited. See California Legislative Analyst's Office, "SB 1 Has Doubled Major Source of State Funding for Local Streets and Roads," January 24, 2020, available at https://perma.cc/GT95-53U4.

78. Paul G. Lewis and Elisa Barbour, *California Cities and the Local Sales Tax* (San Francisco: Public Policy Institute of California, 1999), available at https://perma.cc/UU75-3HAC.

79. In an era of COVID shutdowns, Amazon.com, and dying malls, most local officials likely recognize that there already are limits to the growth of retail sales from brick-and-mortar stores. Thus, the local government favoritism toward retail that was

apparent in past decades may well be less significant today, and the potential pool of future growth in sales tax revenues likely is limited.

80. Oliver P. Williams, *Metropolitan Political Analysis: A Social Access Approach* (New York: Free Press, 1971).

81. On the importance of the perceived distribution of a policy's costs and benefits, see James Q. Wilson, *The Politics of Regulation* (New York: Basic Books, 1982).

CONCLUSION

1. Eran Razin and Mark Rosentraub, "Are Fragmentation and Sprawl Interlinked? North American Evidence," *Urban Affairs Review* 35, no. 6 (2000): pp. 821–836.

2. See, for example, John R. Logan and Harvey L. Molotch, *Urban Fortunes: The Political Economy of Place* (Berkeley: University of California Press, 1987); Stephen L. Elkin, *City and Regime in the American Republic* (Chicago: University of Chicago Press, 1987); David Harvey, "From Managerialism to Entrepreneurialism: The Transformation in Urban Governance in Late Capitalism," *Geografiska Annaler* 71 (1989): pp. 3–17.

3. Michael Manville and Paavo Monkkonen, "Unwanted Housing: Localism and Politics of Housing Development," *Journal of Planning Education and Research* (forthcoming, online 2021): p. 9 (in-text citations omitted).

4. Manville and Monkkonen, p. 4.

5. Liyi Liu, Doug McManus, and Elias Yannopoulos, "Geographic and Temporal Variation in Housing Filtering Rates," *Regional Science and Urban Economics* 93 (2022): pp. 1–36.

6. California Legislative Analyst's Office, *California's High Housing Costs: Causes and Consequences*, March 17, 2015, available at https://perma.cc/R6YB-B3LP; McKinsey Global Institute, *A Tool Kit to Close California's Housing Gap: 3.5 Million Homes by 2025*, October 2016, available at https://perma.cc/9AUK-P899. For a recent example focused on the Bay Area, see SPUR, *What It Will Really Take to Create an Affordable Bay Area* (San Francisco, CA: SPUR, March 2020), available at https://perma.cc/MX7M-SXJ2.

7. See Carolina Reid, *The Costs of Affordable Housing Production: Insights from California's 9% Low-Income Housing Tax Credit Program* (Berkeley, CA: Terner Center for Housing Innovation, 2020), available at https://perma.cc/9LJA-P2YF.

8. Jerusalem Demsas, "America's Racist Housing Rules Really Can Be Fixed," *Vox*, February 17, 2021, available at https://perma.cc/6WYH-5QVK; David Schleicher, "Exclusionary Zoning's Confused Defenders," *Wisconsin Law Review* 2021, no. 5 (2021): pp. 1315–1372; David Schleicher, "Constitutional Law for NIMBYs: A Review of 'Principles of Home Rule for the 21st Century' by the National League of Cities," *Ohio State Law Journal* 81, no. 5 (2020): pp. 883–922.

9. Local Solutions Support Center, "The Threat of State Preemption," available at https://perma.cc/LVN7-433S, accessed on March 9, 2022; Richard Schragger, *City Power: Urban Governance in a Global Age* (New York: Oxford University Press, 2016); on land use, see Richard Schragger, "Local Control of Land Use: A Partial Defense," *State & Local Government Law Blog*, February 17, 2022, available at https://perma.cc/987W-7968.

10. William W. Buzbee, "Asymmetrical Regulation: Risk, Preemption, and the Floor/Ceiling Distinction," *New York University Law Review* 82, no. 6 (2007): pp. 1547–1619.

11. Manville and Monkkonen, "Unwanted Housing," pp. 9–13.

12. John Kingdon, *Agendas, Alternatives, and Public Policies*, 2nd ed. (New York: Pearson, 2010), describes policy change as a process of "coupling" societal problems with preformulated solutions.

13. Joël Thibert, *Governing Urban Regions through Collaboration: A View from North America* (New York: Routledge, 2016), chap. 4, e-book (emphasis in original).

14. Craig Powell, "The Regionalist: Under Steinberg, Will Consolidations Be in Our Future?," *Eye on Sacramento*, 2017, pp. 2–3, available at https://perma.cc/V3J4-9VP5.

15. Taylor, *Shaping the Metropolis.*

16. See, e.g., "California Ends Single-Family Zoning," *The Economist*, September 23, 2021, available at https://perma.cc/CA3M-6T7E.

17. State of California, Department of Justice, Office of the Attorney General, Proposed Initiative 21-0016 (Amdt. #1), 2021, available at https://perma.cc/6TK6-SS38; see also, James Brasuell, "Ballot Initiative Could Overturn California's Zoning Reforms," *Planetizen*, February 15, 2022, available at https://perma.cc/9DVX-HUBC.

18. Andrea Louise Campbell, "Policy Makes Mass Politics," *Annual Review of Political Science* 15, no. 1 (2012): pp. 333–351, at 336.

19. Jacob Hacker and Paul Pierson, "Policy Feedback in an Age of Polarization," *Annals of the American Academy of Political and Social Science* 685 (2019): pp. 8–28; Suzanne Mettler, "Bringing the State Back in to Civic Engagement: Policy Feedback Effects of the G.I. Bill for World War II Veterans," *American Political Science Review* 96, no. 2 (2002): pp. 351–365; Frank Baumgartner and Bryan Jones, *Agendas and Instability in American Politics*, rev. ed. (Chicago: University of Chicago Press, 2009).

TECHNICAL APPENDIX

1. For discussion of the statistical areas used in our analysis, see Office of Management and Budget, "Revised Delineations of Metropolitan Statistical Areas, Micropolitan Statistical Areas, and Combined Statistical Areas, and Guidance on Uses of the Delineations of These Areas," 2015, available at https://perma.cc/TTJ5-HWQN.

2. For the definition of "urbanized area," see 76 Fed. Reg. 53030, 53039 (2011).

3. We improve reliability of the estimates by combining multiple estimates to produce our dependent variable, aggregating estimates for the counts of units in buildings with five to nine units, ten to nineteen units, twenty to forty-nine units, and fifty or more units. (For more information on this empirical strategy, see David C. Folch et al., "Spatial Variation in the Quality of American Community Survey Estimates," *Demography* 53, no. 5 (2016): pp. 1535–1554.) Using variance replicate tables provided by the Census Bureau, we calculate a standard error (SE) and coefficient of variation (CV) for each aggregated 2014–2018 estimate. The CV divides the SE for an estimate by the estimate itself. (Where both the numerator and the denominator equal zero, we treat the CV as zero, rather than undefined.) CVs under 0.12 are widely understood to indicate high reliability; CVs between 0.12 and 0.4 typically indicate moderate reliability (p. 1539). Here, our sample includes only the high-reliability estimates, but we attained substantially similar results when running the regression with samples including the moderate-reliability estimates.

Index

Sacramento region, 81
Sales tax, 34, 41, 65–67, 71t, 91n13, 104–105n79
San Bernardino County, 61
San Francisco, City and County of, 2, 11, 13, 26, 28–29, 35, 46, 75, 89n5, 95n20, 100n21; Board of Supervisors, 29; unified city-county government, 48, 98n6
San Francisco Bay, 33, 50–51, 80–81
San Francisco Bay Area: difficulty of designing elected regional government for, 60, 69; filtering up of housing in, 78; geographic definition of, 3f, 89n5; governmental structure of, 2, 4–7, 13–19, 25, 40, 46–48, 76; housing market characteristics, 1, 7–8, 26–27, 30, 61; in-commuting from outside of region, 3f, 51, 76, 89n5; multi-centric development of, 13–14, 46; suburbanization of, 10–14, 31; region-wide policy dilemmas, 56; values and priorities of public, 43. See also Race and racism; Regional agencies; Regional governmental structure
San Joaquin County, 3f, 31, 89n5
San Joaquin Valley, 31, 51, 76
San Jose, City of, 2, 11, 25, 28–29, 46, 75, 98–99n7, 100n21
San Mateo County, 13, 26, 45, 89n5, 95n20, 98n6
Santa Clara County, 26, 30, 45, 48, 89n5, 95n20, 96n35
Schafran, Alex, 13
School districts, 14–19, 67, 71t
School quality, 8–9, 13, 16
Scope of conflict, 9, 83, 91n9
Segregation. See Race and racism
Silicon Valley, 26, 46. See also San Mateo County; Santa Clara County
Small-scale cities. See Jurisdictional size
Social housing, 78–79
Social Security, 83
Sonoma County, 36, 55, 89n5
Southern California Association of Governments, 51
South of Market neighborhood (San Francisco), 28–29

Special districts, 14–18, 32–33, 38, 48, 52, 57–59, 67, 81, 93n33, 96n25, 101n35
Sprawl, 16, 22, 30–33, 36, 54, 59, 68–69, 76, 82
Stanislaus County, 31
State government. See California state government
Structure of government. See Regional governmental structure
Subdivision regulations, 2, 15–16

Taylor, Zack, 82, 102n38
Taxation. See Gasoline tax; Property tax; Sales tax
Tech workers, 7, 78
Tenants. See Renters
Thibert, Joël, 80
Torlakson, Tom, 36–37, 97n37
Transit-adjacent development, 2–5, 29, 32–33, 37–38, 41, 53, 58–59, 69, 78, 90n8
Tranter, Revan, 34, 36
Twin Cities Metropolitan Council, 102n38

Undeveloped land, 11, 15, 21–22, 24, 65. See also Open space
Unincorporated areas, 15–16, 24, 46–47, 89n4, 98–99nn7–8
University of California, Berkeley, 13, 36, 55
Urban growth boundary, 58–59
Use value, 77

Vacant land. See Undeveloped land
Vallejo, City of, 11
Vance, James, 13–14

West Oakland neighborhood, 29–30

YIMBY ("Yes in My Backyard"). See Prohousing

Zoning, 2, 7–8, 10–13, 15–16, 21, 26–28, 31–32, 38–39, 41, 45, 53, 56–57, 59–67, 70–71t, 77–78, 82; enabling legislation in California, 92n16; exclusionary, 73, 79; override of, 62–64, 103n54

Paul G. Lewis is Associate Professor in the School of Politics and Global Studies at Arizona State University. His previous books include *Shaping Suburbia: How Political Institutions Organize Urban Development, Custodians of Place: Governing the Growth and Development of Cities,* and *Policing Immigrants: Local Law Enforcement on the Front Lines.*

Nicholas J. Marantz is Associate Professor in the Department of Urban Planning and Public Policy at the University of California, Irvine.